W9-DJE-296

UNDERSTANDING FINANCIAL STATEMENTS
Through the Maze of a Corporate Annual Report

UNDERSTANDING FINANCIAL STATEMENTS
Through the Maze of a Corporate Annual Report

Lyn M. Fraser
Texas A & M University

Reston Publishing Company, Inc.
A Prentice-Hall Company
Reston, Virginia

Library of Congress Cataloging in Publication Data

Fraser, Lyn M.
    Understanding financial statements.

    1. Financial statements.   2. Corporation reports.
I. Title.
HF5681.B2F764   1985   657'.33   84–11641
ISBN 0-8359-8042-1 (C)
ISBN 0-8359-8041-3 (P)

© 1985 by Reston Publishing Company, Inc.
    A Prentice-Hall Company
    Reston, Virginia

10   9   8   7   6   5   4   3   2   1

Printed in the United States of America

For Don and Eleanor
And in memory of my father

Contents

Preface

The objective of this book is to present the conceptual background and analytical tools necessary to understand and interpret financial statements. The material included in the book has evolved from many classroom hours spent during the last five years teaching a course in financial statement analysis to graduate and undergraduate students and from presentations to business groups on the topic of analyzing financial statements.

It is hoped that the book will be useful for a wide variety of purposes:

- as a textbook or supplementary textbook for courses in financial statement analysis, investments, corporate finance, principles of accounting and general business studies

- for continuing education courses and executive development programs covering the understanding and interpretation of corporate financial statements

- as a reference book for credit analysts, investment analysts, stock brokers, and others who make decisions based on the analysis of financial statements

- for those having an interest in specialized areas of financial reporting, such as the importance of cash flow from operations as a performance measure; the impact of inflation on financial statements; the analysis of a business firm's operations by segment; and the effect of choices and changes in accounting policies on financial statements

- as a guidebook on corporate financial statements for investors, managers, and the general public.

The author would like to acknowledge those who have contributed to the completion of the book and (hopefully) to upgrading its quality.

First, I would like to thank my many students who have aided—through questions, comments, discussions, and responses—the development of many of the ideas and examples presented in the book.

Grateful appreciation is expressed to Aileen Ormiston, CPA, for her invaluable help and support in each stage of the planning and writing of the book. I am particularly appreciative of her suggestions on the original draft of the manuscript, her attention to detail, *and* her sense of humor.

Several persons have provided critical reviews of the text. Especially helpful were the comments received from Dr. Gene C. Uselton, Texas A&M University; G. Mark Simmons, Sam Houston State University; Dr. Donald R. Fraser, Texas A&M University; Dr. Carl M. Guelzo, Catonsville Community College; John Renford Taylor, President, North Central Bank, Austin, Texas; and Dr. Grant J. Wells, Ball State University.

I owe a special debt of gratitude to my running friends for keeping me (relatively) sane.

Finally, I would like to thank my husband Don and my daughter Eleanor for their patience and encouragement.

LYN M. FRASER

UNDERSTANDING FINANCIAL STATEMENTS
Through the Maze of a Corporate Annual Report

Introduction

Have you ever picked up a corporate annual report, flipped through the glossy pictures and colorful charts, and then turned expectantly (or perhaps reluctantly) to the financial statements only to find them incomprehensible?

- Have you had suspicions that management was manipulating, or at least massaging, the financial statement numbers in order to make the company look better?

- Have you read articles or heard discussions about topics such as "cash flow vs. net income," or "the switch to lifo," and wondered what they meant?

- Do you have an interest in learning more about financial statements for a specific purpose, such as making an investment or credit decision about a company?

- Do you need a greater understanding of financial statements in order to advance professionally?

If the answer to any of the preceding questions is yes, then this book should be beneficial to you. If the answer is no, then surely we can think of additional questions to elicit a positive response, such as: Will the material in this book help you pass an examination or a course?

The purpose of this book is to convey information about how to read and evaluate corporate financial statements and to present the material in a straight-forward manner that will be easy to follow and understandable to any reader, regardless of background or perspective. The book is written for anyone who wants to learn more about the content and interpretation of financial statements. The reader can expect more than a dull exposition of financial data and accounting rules. Throughout these pages we will attempt to get behind the numbers and accounting policies to uncover how well companies—not their accountants—are really doing. The financial statements should facilitate, rather than hinder, our progress.

The following chapters show how to extract useful information from a corporate annual report. Although the illustrations are based on corporate reporting, the discussion also applies to financial statements of small business firms that use generally accepted accounting principles.

Obstacles to Understanding Financial Statements

1. Volume of information in a corporate annual report.

2. Complexity of the accounting rules that underly the preparation and presentation of financial statements.

3. Potential for management to manipulate financial statement presentation and affect the quality of financial reporting.

4. Distortion of financial statements caused by inflation.

5. Important financial information that is omitted or difficult to find.

ORGANIZATION Chapter 1 provides an overview of financial statements and presents some of the difficulties one encounters in attempting to make sense of the numbers and notes. These problems include the volume and complexity of the data, the potential for management manipulation, the distortions caused by inflation, and the omission of key information.

Chapters 2 through 5 cover the description and analysis of financial statements for a mythical but potentially real company: Recreational Equipment and Clothing, Incorporated (R.E.C., Inc.), which sells recreational products through retail outlets in the southwestern area of the United States. The specifics of this particular firm should be helpful in illustrating how financial statement analysis can provide insight into a firm's strengths and weaknesses. But the principles and concepts covered throughout the book apply to any set of published financial statements (other than for specialized industries, such as banking, public utilities, or real estate). Chapters 2 through 4 discuss in detail a basic set of financial statements: the balance sheet (Chapter 2); the income and retained earnings statements (Chapter 3); and the statement of changes in financial position (Chapter 4). The focus is on what the financial statements convey as well as how the numbers have been derived. With this material as background, Chapter 5 covers the interpretation and analysis of financial statements. This process involves the calculation and interpretation of financial ratios, an examination of trends over time, a comparison of the firm's condition and performance with its competitors, and an assessment of the future potential of the company based on its historical record.

Appendix A presents a comprehensive illustration of how management can influence the outcome of financial statement numbers through changes in accounting policies. The impact of inflation on financial statements is covered in Appendix B; and Appendix C shows how to analyze the segmental financial data of diversified companies.

Self-tests at the ends of Chapters 2, 3, 4, and 5 provide an opportunity to assess comprehension (or its absence!) of each major topic, with solutions provided in Appendix D.

A list of key financial ratios and definitions of important terms used throughout the book are presented in Appendix E and Appendix F.

The ultimate goal of this book is to improve the reader's ability to translate financial statement numbers into meaningful tools for business decisions. It is hoped that the material covered will enable each reader to approach corporate financial statements with greater confidence concerning their usefulness.

Figure I.1

R.E.C. Inc.
1983 Annual Report

Exhibit I.1   R.E.C., Inc.
Consolidated Balance Sheets at December 31, 1983 and 1982
(In thousands)

	1983	1982
Assets		
Current Assets		
Cash	$ 4,061	$ 2,382
Marketable securities (note A)	5,272	8,004
Accounts receivable, less allowance for doubtful accounts of $448 in 1983		
and $417 in 1982	8,960	8,350
Inventories (note A)	47,041	36,769
Prepaid expenses	512	759
Total current assets	65,846	56,264
Property, Plant and Equipment (notes A, C, and E)		
Land	811	811
Buildings and leasehold improvements	18,273	11,928
Equipment	21,523	13,768
	40,607	26,507
Less accumulated depreciation and amortization	11,528	7,530
Net property, plant and equipment	29,079	18,977
Other Assets (note A)	373	668
Total Assets	$95,298	$75,909
Liabilities and Stockholders' Equity		
Current Liabilites		
Accounts payable	$14,294	$7,591
Notes payable—banks (note B)	5,614	6,012
Current maturities of long-term debt (note C)	1,884	1,516
Accrued liabilities	5,669	5,313
Total current liabilities	27,461	20,432
Deferred Federal Income Taxes (notes A and D)	843	635
Long-Term Debt (note C)	21,059	16,975
Total liabilities	49,363	38,042
Stockholders' Equity		
Common stock, par value $1, authorized, 10,000,000 shares; issued,		
4,803,000 shares in 1983 and 4,594,000 shares in 1982 (note F)	4,803	4,594
Additional paid-in capital	957	910
Retained earnings	40,175	32,363
Total stockholders' equity	45,935	37,867
Total Liabilities and Stockholders' Equity	$95,298	$75,909

The accompanying notes are an integral part of these statements.

R.E.C., Inc.
Consolidated Statements of Earnings and Retained Earnings
For the Years ended December 31, 1983, 1982, and 1981
(In thousands except per share amounts)

Exhibit I.1
(Continued)

	1983	1982	1981
Statements of Consolidated Earnings			
Net sales	$215,600	$153,000	$140,700
Cost of goods sold (note A)	129,364	91,879	81,606
Gross profit	86,236	61,121	59,094
Selling and administrative expenses (note A)	32,664	26,382	25,498
Advertising	14,258	10,792	9,541
Lease payments (note E)	13,058	7,111	7,267
Depreciation and amortization (note A)	3,998	2,984	2,501
Repairs and maintenance	3,015	2,046	3,031
Operating profit	19,243	11,806	11,256
Other income (expense)			
Interest income	422	838	738
Interest expense	(2,585)	(2,277)	(1,274)
Earnings before income taxes	17,080	10,367	10,720
Income taxes (notes A and D)	7,686	4,457	4,824
Net Earnings	$ 9,394	$ 5,910	$ 5,896
Earnings per common share (note G)	$1.96	$1.29	$1.33
Statements of Consolidated Retained Earnings			
Retained earnings at beginning of year	$ 32,363	$ 28,315	$ 24,260
Net earnings	9,394	5,910	5,896
Cash dividends (1983—$.33 per share; 1982 and 1981— $.41 per share)	(1,582)	(1,862)	(1,841)
Retained earnings at end of year	$ 40,175	$ 32,363	$ 28,315

The accompanying notes are an integral part of these statements.

Exhibit I.1
(Continued)

R.E.C., Inc.
Consolidated Statements of Changes in Financial Position
For the years ended December 31, 1983, 1982, and 1981
(In thousands)

	1983	1982	1981
Sources of working capital			
From operations			
Net earnings for the year	$ 9,394	$ 5,910	$5,896
Charges to earnings not using working capital			
Depreciation and amortization (note A)	3,998	2,984	2,501
Deferred income taxes—noncurrent (notes A and D)	208	136	118
Working Capital provided from operations	13,600	9,030	8,515
Additions to long-term debt	5,600	7,882	629
Sales of common stock	256	183	124
Other sources	295	—	—
Total Sources	19,751	17,095	9,268
Uses of working capital			
Additions to property, plant and equipment	14,100	4,773	3,982
Reductions of long-term debt	1,516	1,593	127
Cash dividends	1,582	1,862	1,841
Total Uses	17,198	8,228	5,950
Increase in Working Capital	$ 2,553	$ 8,867	$3,318
Changes in components of working capital			
Increase (decrease) in current assets			
Cash	$ 1,679	(235)	$ 782
Marketable securities	(2,732)	(1,841)	976
Accounts receivable—net	610	3,339	448
Inventories	10,272	7,006	2,331
Prepaid expenses	(247)	(295)	82
	9,582	7,974	4,619
Increase (decrease) in current liabilities			
Accounts payable	6,703	(1,051)	902
Notes payable—banks	(398)	1,931	1,452
Current maturities of long-term debt	368	(77)	(126)
Accrued liabilities	356	(1,696)	(927)
	7,029	(893)	1,301
Increase in Working Capital	$ 2,553	$ 8,867	$3,318

The accompanying notes are an integral part of these statements.

R.E.C., Inc.
Notes to Consolidated Financial Statements
December 31, 1983, December 31, 1982, and December 31, 1981

Exhibit I.1
(Continued)

Note A—Summary of Significant Accounting Policies

R.E.C., Inc. is a retailer of recreational equipment and clothing.

Consolidation: The consolidated financial statements include the accounts and transactions of the company and its wholly-owned subsidiaries. The company accounts for its investment in its subsidiaries using the equity method of accounting. All significant intercompany transactions have been eliminated in consolidation.

Marketable securities: Marketable securities consist of short-term, interest-bearing securities stated at cost, which approximates market.

Inventories: Inventories are stated at the lower of cost (LIFO) or market. If the first-in, first-out (FIFO) method of inventory accounting had been used, inventories would have been approximately $2,681,000 and $2,096,000 higher than reported at December 31, 1983 and 1982.

Depreciation and Amortization: Property, plant, and equipment is stated at cost. Depreciation expense is calculated principally by the straight-line method based on estimated useful lives of 3 to 10 years for equipment, 3 to 30 years for leasehold improvements, and 40 years for buildings. Estimated useful lives of leasehold improvements represent the remaining term of the lease in effect at the time the improvements are made.

Income Taxes: Deferred income taxes are provided for timing differences between earnings for financial reporting and income tax purposes. The timing differences are principally related to accelerated tax depreciation and use of the installment method for tax purposes on contract and charge sales. Investment tax credits are accounted for by the flow-through method, which recognizes the credits in the period in which they arise.

Expenses of New Stores: Expenses associated with the opening of new stores are charged to expense as incurred.

Other Assets: Other assets are investments in properties not used in business operations.

Note B—Short-Term Debt

The company has a $10,000,000 bank line of credit. Interest is calculated at the prime rate plus 1% on any outstanding balance. Any balance on March 31, 1985, converts to a term note payable in quarterly installments over 5 years.

Note C—Long-Term Debt

Long-term debt consists of the following at the end of each year:

	1983	1982
Mortgage notes collateralized by land and buildings (approximate cost of $7,854,000) payable in aggregate monthly installments of $30,500 plus interest at 8¾–10½% maturing from 1999–2012	$ 3,808,000	$ 4,174,000
Unsecured promissory note due December, 1995, payable in quarterly installments of $100,000 plus interest at 8½%	4,800,000	5,200,000
Promissory notes secured by equipment (approximate cost of $9,453,000) payable in semiannual installments of $375,000 plus interest at 13%, due in January, 1992	6,000,000	6,750,000
Unsecured promissory note payable in three installments of $789,000 in 1985, 1986, and 1987, plus interest at 9¼% payable annually	2,367,000	2,367,000
Promissory notes secured by equipment (approximate cost of $8,546,000) payable in annual installments of $373,000 plus interest at 12½% due in June, 1999	5,968,000	—
	22,943,000	18,491,000
Less current maturities	1,884,000	1,516,000
	$21,059,000	$16,975,000

Exhibit I.1
(Continued)

Current maturities for each of the following five years are:

December 31, 1984	$2,678,000
1985	2,678,000
1986	2,678,000
1987	1,884,000
1988	1,884,000

Note D—Income Taxes

A reconciliation of income tax expense computed by using the statutory Federal income tax rate and the amount of income tax expense reported in the consolidated statements of earnings is as follows:

	1983	1982	1981
Federal income tax at statutory rate	$7,859,000	$4,769,000	$4,931,000
Increases (decreases)			
State income taxes	489,000	381,000	344,000
Investment tax credits	(465,000)	(429,000)	(228,000)
Other items, net	(197,000)	(264,000)	(223,000)
Income Tax expense reported	$7,686,000	$4,457,000	$4,824,000

Deferred tax expense applicable to major timing differences is as follows:

	1983	1982	1981
Excess of tax depreciation over book depreciation	$146,000	$ 98,000	$ 84,000
Timing differences applicable to installment sales	62,000	38,000	34,000
Total	$208,000	$136,000	$118,000

Note E—Operating Leases

The company conducts some of its operations in facilities leased under noncancellable operating leases. Certain agreements include options to purchase the property and certain agreements include renewal options with provisions for increased rental during the renewal term.

Minimum annual rental commitments as of December 31, 1983, are as follows:

1984	$ 14,561,000
1985	14,082,000
1986	13,673,000
1987	13,450,000
1988	13,003,000
Thereafter	107,250,000
	$176,019,000

Note F—Common Stock

The company has a stock option plan providing that options may be granted to key employees at an option price of not less than 100% of the market value of the shares at the time the options are granted. As of December 31, 1983, the company has under option 75,640 shares (1982—96,450 shares). All options expire 5 years from date of grant.

Note G—Earnings Per Share

Earnings per common share are based on the weighted average number of common shares outstanding during each year. For 1983, 1982, and 1981 the weighted average number of common shares outstanding was 4,792,857, 4,581,395, and 4,433,083, respectively. Outstanding options are included in periods where they have a dilutive effect. Earnings per share assuming full dilution are not significantly different (less than 3%) from earnings per common share.

Auditor's Report

Exhibit I.1
(Continued)

Board of Directors and Stockholders
R.E.C., Inc.

We have examined the consolidated balance sheets of R.E.C., Inc. and subsidiaries as of December 31, 1983 and 1982, and the related consolidated statements of earnings, retained earnings, and changes in financial position for each of the 3 years in the period ended December 31, 1983. Our examinations were made in accordance with generally accepted auditing standards and, accordingly, included such tests of the accounting records and such other auditing procedures as we considered necessary in the circumstances.

In our opinion, the financial statements referred to above present fairly the consolidated financial position of R.E.C., Inc. and subsidiaries at December 31, 1983 and 1982, and the consolidated results of their operations and changes in their financial position for each of the 3 years in the period ended December 31, 1983, in conformity with generally accepted accounting principles applied on a consistent basis.

J. J. Michaels and Company
Donelyn, Texas
January 27, 1984

The Maze of Corporate **1** Financial Statements

maze (māz), *n.* 1. a confusing intricate network of passages, some blind and some leading to a goal. 2. something intricately or confusingly elaborate or complicated.

The words used to define "maze" could also be applied to "financial statements." The typical set of financial statements found in corporate annual reports for publicly held companies in the United States contains a wealth of useful information regarding the financial position of the firm, the success of its operations, the policies and strategies of management, and insight into its

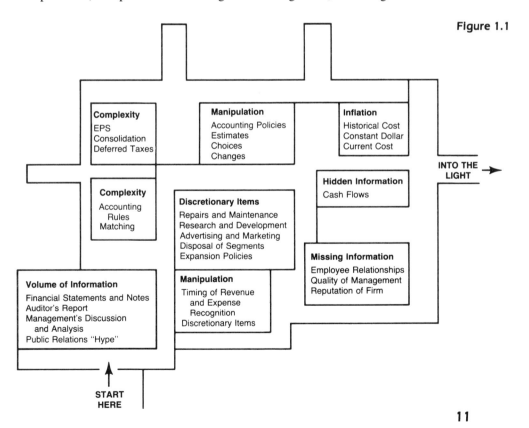

Figure 1.1

future performance.[1] The objective of the financial statement user is to find and interpret this information in order to answer questions about the company, such as the following:

- Would an investment generate attractive returns?
- Should existing investment holdings be liquidated?
- Can the firm repay interest and principal on borrowed funds?
- Does the firm provide a suitable opportunity for employment?
- How well does the company compete in its industry?
- Is this firm a good prospect as a customer?

The financial statements and other materials in a corporate annual report can help answer such questions. The successful search, however, frequently involves overcoming many obstacles in the maze of financial statement data. The user must navigate an intricate network of passages that are frequently confusing and complicated; the path may lead to blocked passages or blind alleys. What are some of these obstacles in the maze of a corporate annual report?

OBSTACLES TO UNDERSTANDING FINANCIAL STATEMENTS

The user of published financial statements can expect to confront an overwhelming volume of financial information that is both included in and supplementary to the statements. The typical corporate annual report contains a set of four basic financial statements (Exhibit 1.1).

Volume of Information

1. The balance sheet shows the financial position of the firm on a particular date.
2. The income or earnings statement presents the results of operations for a period.
3. The statement of retained earnings, which is frequently combined with the income statement, reconciles the beginning and ending balance of the company's retained earnings account. Some firms prepare a more comprehensive statement of shareholders' equity, which reconciles the beginning and ending balance of all equity accounts including retained earnings.
4. The statement of changes in financial position summarizes a firm's financing and investment activities for a period.

Each of these statements will be described and discussed in detail in later sections of the book.

---

1. Annual reports in this book will refer to those published primarily for shareholders and the general public. The Securities and Exchange Commission requires large, publicly held companies to file annually a 10-K report, which is generally a more detailed document. The basic set of financial statements is the same for both types of reports.

Exhibit 1.1

R.E.C. Inc.
1983 Annual Report

Exhibit 1.1
(Continued)

R.E.C., Inc.

Consolidated Balance Sheets at December 31, 1983 and 1982

(In thousands)

	1983	1982
Assets		
Current Assets		
Cash	$ 4,061	$ 2,382
Marketable securities (note A)	5,272	8,004
Accounts receivable, less allowance for doubtful accounts of $448 in 1983 and $417 in 1982	8,960	8,350
Inventories (note A)	47,041	36,769
Prepaid expenses	512	759
Total current assets	65,846	56,264
Property, Plant and Equipment (notes A, C, and E)		
Land	811	811
Buildings and leasehold improvements	18,273	11,928
Equipment	21,523	13,768
	40,607	26,507
Less accumulated depreciation and amortization		
Net property, plant and equipment	11,528	7,530
	29,079	18,977
Other Assets (note A)	373	668
Total Assets	$95,298	$75,909
Liabilities and Stockholders' Equity		
Current Liabilites		
Accounts payable	$14,294	$7,591
Notes payable—banks (note B)	5,614	6,012
Current maturities of long-term debt (note C)	1,884	1,516
Accrued liabilities	5,669	5,313
Total current liabilities	27,461	20,432
Deferred Federal Income Taxes (notes A and D)	843	635
Long-Term Debt (note C)	21,059	16,975
Total liabilities	49,363	38,042
Stockholders' Equity		
Common stock, par value $1, authorized, 10,000,000 shares; issued, 4,803,000 shares in 1983 and 4,594,000 shares in 1982 (note F)	4,803	4,594
Additional paid-in capital	957	910
Retained earnings	40,175	32,363
Total stockholders' equity	45,935	37,867
Total Liabilities and Stockholders' Equity	$95,298	$75,909

The accompanying notes are an integral part of these statements.

R.E.C., Inc.
Consolidated Statements of Earnings and Retained Earnings
For the Years ended December 31, 1983, 1982, and 1981
(In thousands except per share amounts)

Exhibit 1.1
(Continued)

	1983	1982	1981
Statements of Consolidated Earnings			
Net sales	$215,600	$153,000	$140,700
Cost of goods sold (note A)	129,364	91,879	81,606
Gross profit	86,236	61,121	59,094
Selling and administrative expenses (note A)	32,664	26,382	25,498
Advertising	14,258	10,792	9,541
Lease payments (note E)	13,058	7,111	7,267
Depreciation and amortization (note A)	3,998	2,984	2,501
Repairs and maintenance	3,015	2,046	3,031
Operating profit	19,243	11,806	11,256
Other income (expense)			
Interest income	422	838	738
Interest expense	(2,585)	(2,277)	(1,274)
Earnings before income taxes	17,080	10,367	10,720
Income taxes (notes A and D)	7,686	4,457	4,824
Net Earnings	$ 9,394	$ 5,910	$ 5,896
Earnings per common share (note G)	$1.96	$1.29	$1.33
Statements of Consolidated Retained Earnings			
Retained earnings at beginning of year	$ 32,363	$ 28,315	$ 24,260
Net earnings	9,394	5,910	5,896
Cash dividends (1983—$.33 per share; 1982 and 1981— $.41 per share)	(1,582)	(1,862)	(1,841)
Retained earnings at end of year	$ 40,175	$ 32,363	$ 28,315

Immediately following the four financial statements is the section entitled "Notes to the Financial Statements" (Exhibit 1.2). The notes are, in fact, an integral part of the statements and must be read in order to understand the presentation on the face of the financial statements. They explain the firm's accounting policies and provide detail for particular accounts that require clarification. The notes also include information about major acquisitions that have occurred during the accounting period; officer and employee retirement, pension, and stock option plans; the term, cost, and maturity of debt; pending legal proceedings; income taxes and investment tax credits; contingencies and commitments; and quarterly results of operations. Certain supplementary information is required in the notes by the governmental and accounting authorities that establish accounting policies.[2] There are, for instance, extensive supple-

---

2. Primarily the Securities and Exchange Commission and the Financial Accounting Standards Board.

Exhibit 1.1
(Continued)

R.E.C., Inc.
Consolidated Statements of Changes in Financial Position
For the years ended December 31, 1983, 1982, and 1981
(In thousands)

	1983	1982	1981
Sources of working capital			
From operations			
Net earnings for the year	$ 9,394	$ 5,910	$5,896
Charges to earnings not using working capital			
Depreciation and amortization (note A)	3,998	2,984	2,501
Deferred income taxes—noncurrent (notes A and D)	208	136	118
Working Capital provided from operations	13,600	9,030	8,515
Additions to long-term debt	5,600	7,882	629
Sales of common stock	256	183	124
Other sources	295	—	—
Total Sources	19,751	17,095	9,268
Uses of working capital			
Additions to property, plant and equipment	14,100	4,773	3,982
Reductions of long-term debt	1,516	1,593	127
Cash dividends	1,582	1,862	1,841
Total Uses	17,198	8,228	5,950
Increase in Working Capital	$ 2,553	$ 8,867	$3,318
Changes in components of working capital			
Increase (decrease) in current assets			
Cash	$ 1,679	(235)	$ 782
Marketable securities	(2,732)	(1,841)	976
Accounts receivable—net	610	3,339	448
Inventories	10,272	7,006	2,331
Prepaid expenses	(247)	(295)	82
	9,582	7,974	4,619
Increase (decrease) in current liabilities			
Accounts payable	6,703	(1,051)	902
Notes payable—banks	(398)	1,931	1,452
Current maturities of long-term debt	368	(77)	(126)
Accrued liabilities	356	(1,696)	(927)
	7,029	(893)	1,301
Increase in Working Capital	$ 2,553	$ 8,867	$3,318

The accompanying notes are an integral part of these statements.

mentary disclosure requirements relating to reserves for companies operating in the oil, gas, or other areas of the extractive industries. Large, publicly traded companies must include in the notes a set of supplementary schedules to account for the impact of inflation. (This topic is covered in Appendix B.) If a firm has several different lines of business, the notes will contain a section to show revenue, expense, operating profit, and capital expenditures for each segment. (The analysis of segmental data is discussed in Appendix C.)

R.E.C., Inc. Exhibit 1.2
Notes to Consolidated Financial Statements
December 31, 1983, December 31, 1982, and December 31, 1981

Note A—Summary of Significant Accounting Policies
R.E.C., Inc. is a retailer of recreational equipment and clothing.

Consolidation: The consolidated financial statements include the accounts and transactions of the company and its wholly-owned subsidiaries. The company accounts for its investment in its subsidiaries using the equity method of accounting. All significant intercompany transactions have been eliminated in consolidation.

Marketable securities: Marketable securities consist of short-term, interest-bearing securities stated at cost, which approximates market.

Inventories: Inventories are stated at the lower of cost (LIFO) or market. If the first-in, first-out (FIFO) method of inventory accounting had been used, inventories would have been approximately $2,681,000 and $2,096,000 higher than reported at December 31, 1983 and 1982.

Depreciation and Amortization: Property, plant, and equipment is stated at cost. Depreciation expense is calculated principally by the straight-line method based on estimated useful lives of 3 to 10 years for equipment, 3 to 30 years for leasehold improvements, and 40 years for buildings. Estimated useful lives of leasehold improvements represent the remaining term of the lease in effect at the time the improvements are made.

Income Taxes: Deferred income taxes are provided for timing differences between earnings for financial reporting and income tax purposes. The timing differences are principally related to accelerated tax depreciation and use of the installment method for tax purposes on contract and charge sales. Investment tax credits are accounted for by the flow-through method, which recognizes the credits in the period in which they arise.

Expenses of New Stores: Expenses associated with the opening of new stores are charged to expense as incurred.

Other Assets: Other assets are investments in properties not used in business operations.

Note B—Short-Term Debt
The company has a $10,000,000 bank line of credit. Interest is calculated at the prime rate plus 1% on any outstanding balance. Any balance on March 31, 1985, converts to a term note payable in quarterly installments over 5 years.

Note C—Long-Term Debt
Long-term debt consists of the following at the end of each year:

	1983	1982
Mortgage notes collateralized by land and buildings (approximate cost of $7,854,000) payable in aggregate monthly installments of $30,500 plus interest at 8¾–10½% maturing from 1999–2012	$ 3,808,000	$ 4,174,000
Unsecured promissory note due December, 1995, payable in quarterly installments of $100,000 plus interest at 8½%	4,800,000	5,200,000
Promissory notes secured by equipment (approximate cost of $9,453,000) payable in semiannual installments of $375,000 plus interest at 13%, due in January, 1992	6,000,000	6,750,000
Unsecured promissory note payable in three installments of $789,000 in 1985, 1986, and 1987, plus interest at 9¼% payable annually	2,367,000	2,367,000
Promissory notes secured by equipment (approximate cost of $8,546,000) payable in annual installments of $373,000 plus interest at 12½% due in June, 1999	5,968,000	—
	22,943,000	18,491,000
Less current maturities	1,884,000	1,516,000
	$21,059,000	$16,975,000

Exhibit 1.2
(Continued)

Current maturities for each of the following five years are:

December 31, 1984	$2,678,000
1985	2,678,000
1986	2,678,000
1987	1,884,000
1988	1,884,000

Note D—Income Taxes

A reconciliation of income tax expense computed by using the statutory Federal income tax rate and the amount of income tax expense reported in the consolidated statements of earnings is as follows:

	1983	1982	1981
Federal income tax at statutory rate	$7,859,000	$4,769,000	$4,931,000
Increases (decreases)			
State income taxes	489,000	381,000	344,000
Investment tax credits	(465,000)	(429,000)	(228,000)
Other items, net	(197,000)	(264,000)	(223,000)
Income Tax expense reported	$7,686,000	$4,457,000	$4,824,000

Deferred tax expense applicable to major timing differences is as follows:

	1983	1982	1981
Excess of tax depreciation over book depreciation	$146,000	$ 98,000	$ 84,000
Timing differences applicable to installment sales	62,000	38,000	34,000
Total	$208,000	$136,000	$118,000

Note E—Operating Leases

The company conducts some of its operations in facilities leased under noncancellable operating leases. Certain agreements include options to purchase the property and certain agreements include renewal options with provisions for increased rental during the renewal term.

Minimum annual rental commitments as of December 31, 1983, are as follows:

1984	$ 14,561,000
1985	14,082,000
1986	13,673,000
1987	13,450,000
1988	13,003,000
Thereafter	107,250,000
	$176,019,000

Note F—Common Stock

The company has a stock option plan providing that options may be granted to key employees at an option price of not less than 100% of the market value of the shares at the time the options are granted. As of December 31, 1983, the company has under option 75,640 shares (1982—96,450 shares). All options expire 5 years from date of grant.

Note G—Earnings Per Share

Earnings per common share are based on the weighted average number of common shares outstanding during each year. For 1983, 1982, and 1981 the weighted average number of common shares outstanding was 4,792,857, 4,581,395, and 4,433,083, respectively. Outstanding options are included in periods where they have a dilutive effect. Earnings per share assuming full dilution are not significantly different (less than 3%) from earnings per common share.

Exhibit 1.3

Auditor's Report

Board of Directors and Stockholders
R.E.C., Inc.

We have examined the consolidated balance sheets of R.E.C., Inc. and subsidiaries as of December 31, 1983 and 1982, and the related consolidated statements of earnings, retained earnings, and changes in financial position for each of the 3 years in the period ended December 31, 1983. Our examinations were made in accordance with generally accepted auditing standards and, accordingly, included such tests of the accounting records and such other auditing procedures as we considered necessary in the circumstances.

In our opinion, the financial statements referred to above present fairly the consolidated financial position of R.E.C., Inc. and subsidiaries at December 31, 1983 and 1982, and the consolidated results of their operations and changes in their financial position for each of the 3 years in the period ended December 31, 1983, in conformity with generally accepted accounting principles applied on a consistent basis.

J. J. Michaels and Company
Donelyn, Texas
January 27, 1984

Related to the financial statements and notes is the report of an independent auditor (Exhibit 1.3). Management has responsibility for the preparation of financial statements, including the notes, and the auditor's report attests to the fairness of the presentation. An ''unqualified'' report states that the financial statements present fairly the financial position, the results of operations, and the changes in financial position for the company. Some circumstances warrant a ''qualified'' opinion; these include the departure from a generally accepted accounting principle, inconsistent application of accounting principles, and uncertainties regarding the outcome of significant matters including factors that might impair the firm's ability to continue as a going concern.

Other material in a corporate annual report may prove helpful to the financial analyst or may simply contribute to the information overload. For example, the report contains a discussion and analysis by management of the company's operating performance and financial condition. There is also a five-year summary of data on operating revenue, profit or loss, total assets, long-term obligations, and cash dividends. Some companies add charts, graphs, and a variety of other additional descriptive items. (The amount of this descriptive public relations type of material sometimes varies inversely with the success of the firm's performance for a particular year!)

Given the quantity of information found in and surrounding the financial statements, it can be difficult to uncover the relevant data needed to make an intelligent and informed decision.

Complexity of Financial Statements

The financial statements themselves are complex and often confusing. The statements are prepared according to generally accepted accounting principles, which provide a measure of uniformity but also allow considerable discretion in the preparation of the statements. Several examples illustrate the potential causes of user confusion.

Figure 1.2

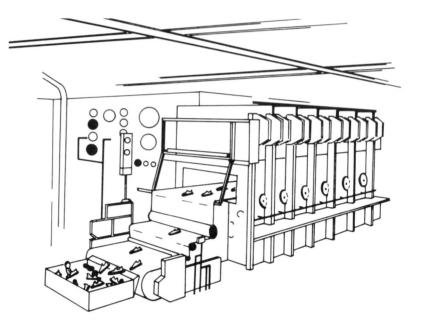

One example involves the depreciation of fixed assets.[3] Fixed assets are those assets such as machinery and equipment, that benefit the firm for several years. When such an asset is acquired, the cost of the asset is allocated or spread over its useful life rather than expensed in the year of purchase. This allocation process is depreciation. Assume that equipment is purchased at a cost of $50,000. Several choices and estimates must be made in order to determine the annual depreciation expense associated with the equipment. Management must estimate how long the equipment will be productive and the amount, if any, of salvage value at the end of its useful life. Further, management must choose a method of depreciation: the straight-line method allocates an equal amount of expense to each year of the depreciation period, while an accelerated method apportions larger amounts of expense to the earlier years of the asset's depreciable life and lesser amounts to the later years. If the $50,000 equipment is estimated to have a five-year useful life and $0 salvage value at the end of that period, annual depreciation expense would be calculated as follows for the first year:

Straight Line:

$$\frac{\text{Depreciable Base (Cost less Salvage Value)}}{\text{Depreciation Period}} = \text{Depreciation Expense}$$

$$\frac{\$50,000 - \$0}{5} = \$10,000$$

3. Also called tangible fixed assets, long-lived assets, and capital assets.

Accelerated[4]:

Cost less Accumulated Depreciation $\times$ Twice the Straight Line Rate $=$
Depreciation Expense

$$50,000 \times (2 \times .2) = \$20,000$$

The choices and estimates relating to the depreciation of equipment affect the amounts shown on the financial statements relating to the asset—the "fixed asset" account on the balance sheet is shown at historical cost less accumulated depreciation; and the annual depreciation expense is deducted on the income statement to determine net income. At the end of year 1, the accounts would be different according to the method chosen:

Straight Line:

Balance Sheet		Income Statement	
Fixed Assets	$50,000	Dep. Expense	$10,000
Less: Accum. Dep.	(10,000)		
Fixed Assets (Net)	$40,000		

Accelerated:

Balance Sheet		Income Statement	
Fixed Assets	$50,000	Dep. Expense	$20,000
Less: Accum. Dep.	(20,000)		
Fixed Assets (Net)	$30,000		

The amounts would also vary if the estimates were different regarding useful life or salvage value. This one example is compounded by all of the firm's depreciable assets and by the other accounts that are affected by accounting methods, for instance the inventory account, which will be discussed in detail in Chapter 2.

Not only are financial statements encumbered by accounting choices and estimates, but they also reflect an attempt to "match" revenues with expenses in appropriate accounting periods. If a firm sells goods on credit, there is a delay between the time the product is sold and the time the cash is collected. Published financial statements are prepared according to the "accrual" rather than the "cash" basis of accounting. This means that the revenue is recognized in the accounting period when the sale is made rather than when the cash is received. The same principle applies to expense recognition; the expense asso-

---

4. The example uses the double-declining balance method, which is: twice the straight-line rate times the net book value (cost less accumulated depreciation) of the asset.

Depreciation expense under each method for year 2 would be:

	Straight Line	Accelerated
Year 2	$\dfrac{\$50,000}{5} = \$10,000$	$\$30,000 \times .4 = \$12,000$

Figure 1.3

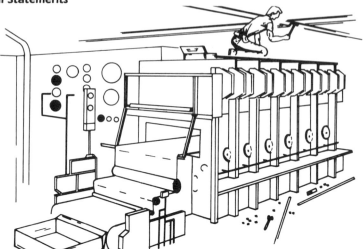

ciated with the product may occur before the cash is actually paid out. The process of matching revenue and expense to accounting periods involves considerable estimation and judgment and, like the depreciation example, affects the outcome of the financial statement numbers. If, for instance, the $50,000 equipment needed major repair in year 2, management would have to determine whether to recognize the cost of repair in year 2 or to spread it over years 2 through 5.

Further, financial statements are prepared on certain dates at the end of accounting periods, such as a quarter or a year. Whereas the firm's life is continuous, financial data must be appropriated to particular time periods.

Because the accounting principles underlying the preparation of financial statements are complicated, the presentation of data based on the accounting rules can be perplexing. One example of a complex accounting rule that sometimes results in confusion is that for the calculation of earnings per share. One typically thinks of earnings per share as the amount of net income earned for every share of common stock outstanding. But the income statement for many companies, those with complex capital structures (which include convertible securities, stock options, and warrants), will show two figures for earnings per share: primary and fully diluted. Convertible securities, stock options, and warrants represent potential "dilution" of earnings per share; that is, if they were exercised there would be more shares of stock outstanding for every dollar earned. The accounting rules require that this potential for dilution be considered in the computation of earnings per share, and the result is a dual presentation. (This topic is discussed more fully in Chapter 3.)

The earnings per share calculation is just one of a vast number of financial statements puzzles. Sorting out the consolidation of a parent and subsidiaries, the accounting for leases and pensions, or the translation of foreign operations of an American company can cause nightmares for the logical financial analyst. One of the most useful documents in a corporate annual report is the Statement of Changes in Financial Position; but this statement is frequently overlooked for lack of understanding its intent and content. (This statement will be described and explained in Chapter 4.)

To add further to the confusion, two sets of accounting rules are used by management—one for reporting purposes (preparation of financial statements for the public) and one for tax purposes (calculation of taxes for the Internal Revenue Service). Earlier in this section there was an example of the choices associated with the depreciation of an asset. Frequently a firm will select different depreciation methods for tax and reporting purposes. The objective of tax accounting is to pay the smallest amount of tax possible; thus, the firm will choose an accelerated method of depreciation to take larger expense deductions in the earlier life of the asset.[5] For reporting purposes, however, the straight-line method is commonly used because it spreads the expense evenly and results in higher reported income in the earlier years. Referring to the previous example, the following results were obtained according to the two depreciation methods for year 1:

Straight Line	Accelerated
Income Statement	Income Statement
Dep. Expense $10,000	Dep. Expense $20,000

Use of the straight-line method produces an expense deduction that is $10,000 less than the accelerated method; net income, therefore, would be $10,000 higher in year 1 under the straight-line method. By using the straight-line method for reporting purposes, the tax actually paid to the IRS would be less than the income tax expense reported in the published income statement because taxable income would be less than reported income.[6] (Eventually this difference would reverse, because in the later years of the asset's useful life, accelerated depreciation would be less than straight line; *the total amount of depreciation taken is the same under both methods*.) To reconcile the difference between the amounts of tax expense, there is an account on the balance sheet called "deferred taxes." This account and its interpretation, discussed in Chapter 2, introduces still another challenge to the financial statement user.

Potential Manipulation by Management and the Quality of Reported Earnings

It has already been pointed out that management has considerable discretion within the overall framework of generally accepted accounting principles. As a result, the potential exists for management to "manipulate" the bottom line (profit or loss) and other accounts in financial statements. Ideally, financial statements should reflect an accurate picture of a company's financial condition and performance. The information should be useful both to assess the past and

---

5. Under the Accelerated Cost Recovery System (ACRS), provided by the Economic Recovery Tax Act of 1981, tax rules specify the rate and time period to be used for accelerated depreciation.

6. For a firm with a 40% marginal tax rate, the difference would be $4,000. (Accelerated depreciation expense less straight line depreciation expense times the marginal tax rate: $[\$20,000 - \$10,000] \times .4 = \$4,000$.)

Figure 1.4

"Another successful year, gentlemen. We broke even on operations and pulled a net profit on accounting procedures."

From WSJ Portfolio, permission—Cartoon Features Syndicate.

predict the future. The sharper and clearer the picture presented through the financial data and the closer that picture is to financial reality, the higher is the quality of the financial statements and reported earnings.[7]

Many opportunities exist for management to affect the quality of financial statements; some illustrations follow.

Accounting Policies, Estimates— Choices and Changes

In preparing financial statements, management makes choices with respect to accounting policies and makes estimations in the applications of those policies. One such choice (other examples will be discussed in subsequent chapters) was covered in the preceding section related to the depreciation of fixed assets. To continue the depreciation example, in choosing a depreciation method, management decides how to allocate the depreciation expense associated with a fixed asset purchase. Assume that the $50,000 equipment purchased is more productive in the early stages of its operating life. Financial reality would argue for the selection of an accelerated depreciation method, which would recognize higher depreciation expense in the early years of its productive period. The fact of inflation would also support accelerated depreciation because rising prices have increased the replacement cost of most assets, resulting in an understatement of depreciation based on historical cost. If, however, management wanted to show higher earnings in the early years, the straight-line method would be selected. Note the difference in depreciation expense recognized for year 1:

Straight Line	**Accelerated**
Income Statement	Income Statement
Dep. Expense $10,000	Dep. Expense $20,000

7. For additional reading on the quality of reported earnings, see L. A. Bernstein and J. G. Siegel, "The Concept of Earnings Quality," *The Financial Analysts Journal,* July-August, 1979.

Remember that the lower the expense, the higher is the reported net income. Therefore, under the straight-line method, net income would be $10,000 higher than with the accelerated method. The choice of depreciation method clearly affects the earnings stream associated with the asset, and it also affects the *quality* of the earnings figure reported. Use of accelerated depreciation would produce earnings of higher quality in this particular situation.

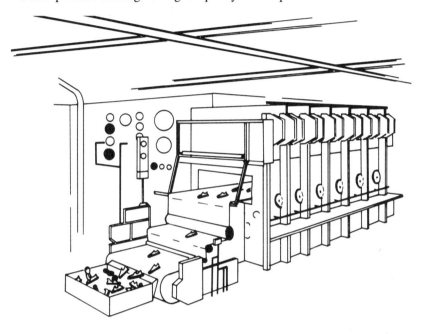

Management can also elect to *change* an accounting policy or estimate if the change can be justified as preferable to what was previously used. In the depreciation example, it was estimated that the equipment had a useful life of five years. It could be argued by management that other firms in the industry depreciate similar assets (classified in an asset group) over a ten-year rather than a five-year period. If the firm had chosen to use the straight-line method and made this accounting change (called a "change in accounting estimate"), depreciation expense would be decreased from $10,000 to $5,000 per year, and net income would increase by $5,000.

Before Change in Estimate		After Change in Estimate	
Income Statement		**Income Statement**	
Dep. Expense	$10,000	Dep. Expense	$5,000

Appendix A presents a comprehensive example illustrating how changes in accounting policies and estimates can affect reported earnings. This appendix will show that for the year 1980, Union Carbide Corporation increased reported earnings by $359 million dollars as a result of several changes in accounting policies and estimates. All of the accounting rules used by Union Carbide were generally accepted accounting principles; there was nothing illegal about the accounting changes, and all were properly disclosed in the notes to the financial statements. Had the changes not been made, however, net income would have dropped between 1979 and 1980 by 4%; the changes boosted 1980 income to $890 million, and there was a *reported* increase in earnings of 60% when compared with 1979. What are the "real" earnings? The reader is referred to Appendix A and to the remainder of this book to help answer that question.

Timing of Revenue and Expense Recognition

One of the generally accepted accounting principles that provides the foundation for the preparation of financial statements is the matching principle: expenses are matched with the generation of revenues in order to determine net income for an accounting period. Reference was made earlier to the fact that published financial statements are based on the "accrual" rather than the "cash" basis of accounting, which means that revenues are recognized when earned and expenses are recognized when incurred, regardless of when the cash inflows or outflows occur. This matching process involves judgments by management regarding the timing of expense and revenue recognition. Although accounting rules provide guidelines helpful in making the necessary and appropriate allocations, these rules are not always precise.

For example, suppose that a company learns near the end of an accounting period that a material accounts receivable is probably uncollectible. When will the account be written off as a loss—currently, or in the next accounting period when a final determination is made? Pose the same question for obsolete inventory sitting on the warehouse shelves gathering dust. These are areas involving sometimes arbitrary managerial decisions. Generally speaking, the more conservative management is in making such judgments (conservatism usually implies the choice that is least favorable to the firm) the higher is the quality of earnings resulting from the matching of revenues and expenses in a given accounting period.

Discretionary Items

Many of the expenditures made by a business firm are discretionary. Management exercises control over the budget levels and timing of expenditures for the repair and maintenance of machinery and equipment, marketing and advertising, research and development, and capital expansion. Policies are also flexible with respect to the replacement of plant assets, the development of new product lines, and the disposal of an operating division. Each choice regarding these discretionary items has both an immediate and long-term impact on profitability, perhaps not in the same direction. A company might elect to defer plant maintenance in order to boost current period earnings; ultimately the effect of such a policy would be detrimental. The American steel industry provides a case in point. Failure to keep pace through adequate maintenance and modernization of plant and equipment has resulted in a severe loss of competitive position and dismal operating performance for the industry as a whole. In the decade through 1980, American production of raw steel as a percentage of

The 10 largest brewers in 1977...   ...and how the top 10 had changed by 1981   Figure 1.5

Data: R.S. Weinberg & Associates, Sanford C. Bernstein & Co., Leading National Advertisers Inc., Radio Advertising Bureau

Reprinted from the July 12, 1982 issue of *Business Week* by special permission, © by McGraw-Hill, Inc.

world production declined from 18.8% to 14.1%, and return on equity for the steel industry was about half of the return posted by the Standard & Poor's 400 industrial stocks.[8]

The nature of a business dictates to a certain extent how discretionary dollars should be spent. For the beer industry, there is a direct relationship between dollars spent for advertising and market share. This relationship is clearly illustrated in Figure 1.5. The dominance of Anheuser-Busch and Miller Brewing Company can be directly attributed to marketing budgets and strategies; Schlitz, on the other hand, has lost ground partly as a result of marketing

---

8. Standard & Poor Corporation's *Industry Surveys,* January, 1983.

decisions.[9] Research and development expenditures are of critical importance to some industries, such as ethical drugs and high technology.

The financial statement analyst should carefully scrutinize managements' policies with respect to these discretionary items through an examination of trends (absolute and relative amounts) and comparison with industry competitors. Such an analysis can provide insight into a company's existing strengths and weaknesses and contribute to an assessment of its ability to perform successfully in the future.

The Impact of Inflation

The historical cost principle of accounting is used to record transactions and to value balance-sheet assets and liabilities. Inventory manufactured or purchased for sale is carried on the balance sheet at cost until a different price is established through an arms-length sales transaction. Buildings, machinery, and equipment are recorded at cost and valued on any balance-sheet date at their original cost less accumulated depreciation. Land used in the business or held for investment also is valued at the original price paid, regardless of any changes in actual market value. Liabilities are measured by the amount of principal balance outstanding.

The historical cost principle correctly and justifiably forms the basis of our accounting system and the preparation of financial statements because it provides an objective and verifiable method of measurement. During a period of inflation, however, distortions occur in the valuation of assets and the determination of net income. Consider the example of the equipment purchased

9. "Anheuser-Busch THE KING OF BEERS STILL RULES," *Business Week,* July 12, 1982.

earlier in this chapter. (Given such heavy illustrative use the equipment will probably be worn out before we reach Chapter 2!) The original purchase price was $50,000, and the equipment was expected to have a five-year useful life. At the end of year 1, using straight-line depreciation, the asset would be valued as follows:

Cost		$50,000
Less:	Accum. Depreciation	10,000
		$40,000

Depreciation expense would be $10,000 for the year. What if, during that year, the general price level had increased by 10%? The replacement cost of the equipment, assuming its price changed at the same rate as the general price level, would now be 10% higher, $50,000 × 1.10 = $55,000, and inflation-adjusted depreciation expense, based on new replacement cost, would be $10,000 × 1.1 = $11,000. If, at the end of 2 years, inflation had continued at a 10% rate, the asset value at replacement cost would be even further from the original cost. Bear in mind that a firm will continue to purchase new assets and replace old ones. The balance sheet "Fixed Assets" category thus reflects assets purchased over many years, with dollars of varying amounts of purchasing power. Because the general price level has risen continuously, there is an annual understatement of depreciation expense and an overstatement of net income for most American companies. Inventory and cost of goods sold can be distorted for the same reasons.

Another problem exists when the general rate of inflation is different from the specific price change for a particular asset, which frequently happens. Land values in many areas have increased at a greater pace than the general price level. On the other hand, prices in some industries, such as high technology, have actually fallen. Both situations cause financial statement distortions. Accountants have been unable to eliminate such distortions and still maintain financial presentations that are objectively determined. The analyst is confronted with the problem of how to extract relevant and reliable figures from conventional financial statements. Although there is no definitive solution, some help is now available.

Large companies are required to present in the notes a supplementary section in which operating income and key balance-sheet and income-statement items are adjusted for the effects of general inflation (the constant-dollar approach) and for specific price changes (the current-cost approach).[10] In particular, net income is adjusted, using both methods, for variations in depreciation expense and cost of goods sold caused by changing prices. This supplementary information can be helpful to the analyst in assessing the impact of inflation on a particular firm's profits and asset valuations. (Appendix B presents an explanation and illustrations of accounting for inflation.)

---

10. Statement of Financial Accounting Standards Number 33, "Financial Reporting and Changing Prices."

Missing and Hidden Information: Where Is Cash Flow?

Some of the facts needed to evaluate a company are not available in the financial statements because they cannot be quantified. These intangibles include employee relations with management, the morale and efficiency of employees, the reputation of the firm with its customers, its prestige in the community, and the quality of management. Often such factors are of considerable importance in making decisions about the worth of a company. A bank might extend credit on the basis of a long-standing relationship with company management and a belief in its ability to weather a difficult period, in spite of what the financial statements show. The employees of Delta Airlines purchased for their company in 1982 a jet airliner and volunteered to take pay cuts in order to help the company through a bad year (Figure 1.6). Certainly this strong and positive relationship between employees and their company is a relevant fact in analyzing the financial statements of Delta Airlines.

Financial statements are general purpose in nature and may not satisfy the particular needs of every user group. For example, an investor attempts to predict the future earnings stream of a company in order to value its securities. The investment analyst would like to have more information than is currently available on the firm's forecast of earnings, its plans for capital expansion, and other such forward-looking material.

Some relevant facts are available in the financial statement numbers but may be difficult for the average reader to find. One such piece of information is *cash flow from operations,* perhaps the most important measure of operating performance. A firm may be extremely successful in terms of sales and profits but may not be generating any cash. How? This topic will be explored in depth in Chapter 4, but a brief preview will be provided here.

Figure 1.6

Delta Receives Gift Plane From Its Employees Today

By a WALL STREET JOURNAL *Staff Reporter*

ATLANTA—A group of Delta Air Line employees has succeeded in its drive to buy the airline a brand new $30 million Boeing Co. 767. The gift, the workers said three months ago, is a sign of general appreciation and of thanks for an 8.5% pay raise the company approved in September.

This morning, with a snip of a blue ribbon, the employees are expected to present the 210-seat, 300,000-pound craft to the company's president, David C. Garrett Jr., and other officials assembled at Atlanta's Hartsfield International Airport. Later in the morning, the 767 known as the ''Spirit of Delta'' is expected to make its inaugural flight from Atlanta to Tampa, Fla.

A spokesman for ''Project 767,'' the employee committee that distributed pledge cards to all 36,000 Delta employees, said about 65% of the employees voluntarily signed the pledges. Most agreed to cut their salaries for a year by 2.5%, he said. The spokesman said the sum of the contributions hasn't yet been totaled but the group is well on its way to the 80% participation rate earlier calculated to cover the aircraft's cost.

Suppose that sales are expanding and that most of the company's sales are on credit. When a sale is recorded, revenue is recognized, and profit is made. But there is also the creation of an accounts receivable. If the quality of customers deteriorates over several years, more and more accounts will prove uncollectible. Thus there can be a year-to-year sales increase and, simultaneously, an even larger rise in accounts receivable. Revenue is recognized for purposes of net income measurement, but all of the sales are not being translated into cash. The company will have to borrow to cover its cash needs and ultimately will face bankruptcy unless the process can be reversed. The giant retailer W.T. Grant went bankrupt for this very reason. Conventional analytical tools did not reveal the extent of its problems until it was too late to salvage the wreckage. However, its cash flow from operations was negative—no internal generation of cash—for all but 2 years of the decade preceding its demise.[11]

Where can you find cash flow? The figure for cash flow from operations is available but usually must be calculated separately from data provided in the Statement of Changes in Financial Position. This calculation, which will be explained in Chapter 4, involves an adjustment of working capital from operations (one of the figures shown in the statement) for net changes in current accounts, such as accounts receivable. Cash flow from operations can be a critically important analytical tool, and one of the purposes of this book is to provide the reader with a clearer understanding of its usefulness.

THROUGH THE MAZE

We are now ready to begin our journey through the maze of corporate financial statements. Negotiating the complex and confusing passages will begin with a step-by-step narration of each financial statement and will conclude with a discussion of what the financial statements reveal about the condition, operating success, and future potential of a company through the analysis and interpretation of the numbers. Although all of the blind alleys and blocked passages cannot be avoided, it is hoped that the reader will learn more about financial statements in order to make sound business decisions.

---

11. J. A. Largay and C. P. Stickney, "Cash Flows, Ratio Analysis, and the W. T. Grant Bankruptcy," *Financial Analysts Journal*, July–August, 1980.

The Balance Sheet 2

Balance sheets are, admittedly, not best-seller reading material. The typical chapter on the balance sheet in most accounting and finance texts is dull at best. This book may be no different in terms of making balance sheets exciting, but we will at least begin by providing some justification for plodding through the statement with a methodical, account-by-account approach.

The balance sheet can teach us a great deal about a business enterprise, particularly when examined over a period of several years and when evaluated in conjunction with the other financial statements. A prerequisite to learning what the balance sheet can teach us, however, is a fundamental understanding of each account and its relationship to the financial statements as a whole. The inventory account is an example. Inventories are an important component of liquidity analysis: can the firm generate sufficient cash to meet cash needs? (This is one of the questions considered in Chapter 5.) Any liquidity ratio[1] that includes inventories will be meaningless without a general understanding of how the balance sheet inventory amount was derived. Thus, Chapter 2 will cover such issues as what inventories are, how the inventory balance is affected by accounting policies, why many companies have shifted to the LIFO method of inventory valuation, where we can find disclosures regarding inventory accounting, and how this one account contributes to the overall measurement of a company's financial condition and operating performance. This step-by-step descriptive treatment of inventories and other balance sheet accounts will provide the background needed to analyze and interpret (the fun part!) the financial statements in Chapter 5.

THE BALANCE SHEET: AN OVERVIEW

The balance sheet, which is sometimes called the "statement of condition" or "statement of financial position," shows the financial condition of a company *on a particular date*. This statement is a summary of what the firm *owns* (assets) and what the firm *owes* to outsiders (liabilities) and to internal owners (stockholders' equity).

$$\text{Assets} = \text{Liabilities} + \text{Stockholders' Equity}$$

---

1. A liquidity ratio (discussed in Chapter 5) measures the ability of a firm to meet needs for cash as they arise; the most commonly used short-term liquidity ratio is the current ratio: current assets ÷ current liabilities.

By definition the balance sheet must balance, that is, the total of all assets must equal the sum of liabilities and stockholders' equity.

In this chapter we will cover account by account the Consolidated Balance Sheet of Recreational Equipment and Clothing, Inc. (R.E.C., Inc.). This particular company sells recreational products through retail outlets, some owned and some leased, in cities located in the southwestern region of the U.S. While the accounts on a balance sheet will vary somewhat by company and by industry, those described in this chapter will be standard for most firms.

EXHIBIT 2.1 **R.E.C., Inc.**
Consolidated Balance Sheets at December 31, 1983 and 1982
(In thousands)

	1983	1982
Assets		
Current Assets		
Cash	$ 4,061	$ 2,382
Marketable securities (note A)	5,272	8,004
Accounts receivable, less allowance for doubtful accounts of $448 in 1983 and $417 in 1982	8,960	8,350
Inventories (note A)	47,041	36,769
Prepaid expenses	512	759
Total current assets	65,846	56,264
Property, Plant and Equipment (notes A, C, and E)		
Land	811	811
Buildings and leasehold improvements	18,273	11,928
Equipment	21,523	13,768
	40,607	26,507
Less accumulated depreciation and amortization	11,528	7,530
Net property, plant and equipment	29,079	18,977
Other Assets (note A)	373	668
Total Assets	$95,298	$75,909
Liabilities and Stockholders' Equity		
Current Liabilites		
Accounts payable	$14,294	$7,591
Notes payable—banks (note B)	5,614	6,012
Current maturities of long-term debt (note C)	1,884	1,516
Accrued liabilities	5,669	5,313
Total current liabilities	27,461	20,432
Deferred Federal Income Taxes (notes A and D)	843	635
Long-Term Debt (note C)	21,059	16,975
Total liabilities	49,363	38,042
Stockholders' Equity		
Common stock, par value $1, authorized, 10,000,000 shares; issued, 4,803,000 shares in 1983 and 4,594,000 shares in 1982 (note F)	4,803	4,594
Additional paid-in capital	957	910
Retained earnings	40,175	32,363
Total stockholders' equity	45,935	37,867
Total Liabilities and Stockholders' Equity	$95,298	$75,909

The accompanying notes are an integral part of these statements.

Note first that the statements are "consolidated" for R.E.C., Inc. and subsidiaries. Where a parent company owns more than 50% of the voting stock of a subsidiary, the financial statements are combined for the companies in spite of the fact that they are separate legal entities. The statements are consolidated because they are *in substance* one company, given the proportion of control by the parent. In the case of R.E.C., Inc., the subsidiaries are wholly owned, which means that the parent controls 100% of the voting shares of the subsidiaries. Where less than 100% ownership exists, there are accounts in the consolidated balance sheet and income statement to reflect the minority interest in net assets and income.

Consolidation

The balance sheet is prepared at a point in time at the end of an accounting period, a year or a quarter. Most companies, like R.E.C., Inc., use the calendar year with the accounting period ending on December 31. Interim statements would also be prepared for each quarter, ending March 31, June 30, and September 30. Some companies adopt a fiscal year ending on a date other than December 31.

Balance Sheet Date

The fact that the balance sheet is prepared on a particular date is significant. For example, cash is the first account listed on the balance sheet and represents the amount of cash on December 31; the amount could be materially different on December 30 or January 1.

Financial statements for only one accounting period would be of limited value because there would be no reference point for determining changes in a company's financial record over time. As part of an integrated disclosure system, the information required in annual reports to shareholders now includes two-year audited balance sheets and three-year audited statements of income and changes in financial position.[2] The balance sheet for R.E.C., Inc. thus shows the condition of the company at December 31, 1983 *and* 1982.

Comparative Data

Assets are segregated on a balance sheet according to how they are utilized. "Current" assets include cash or those assets expected to be converted into cash in one year or one operating cycle, whichever is longer. The operating cycle is the time required to purchase or manufacture inventory, sell the product, and collect the cash. For most companies the operating cycle is less than one year, but in some industries—such as tobacco and wine—it is longer. The designation of "current" refers essentially to those assets that are continually used up and replenished in the ongoing operations of the business. The term *working capital* or net working capital is used to designate the amount by which current assets exceed current liabilities (current assets less current liabilities).

ASSETS

Current Assets

2. Adopted by the Securities and Exchange Commission in 1980.

Exhibit 2.2 R.E.C., Inc.
Consolidated Balance Sheets at December 31, 1983 and 1982
(In thousands)

	1983	1982
Assets		
Current Assets		
Cash	$ 4,061	$ 2,382
Marketable securities (note A)	5,272	8,004
Accounts receivable, less allowance for doubtful accounts of $448 in 1983 and $417 in 1982	8,960	8,350
Inventories (note A)	47,041	36,769
Prepaid expenses	512	759
Total current assets	65,846	56,264
Property, Plant and Equipment (notes A, C, and E)		
Land	811	811
Buildings and leasehold improvements	18,273	11,928
Equipment	21,523	13,768
	40,607	26,507
Less accumulated depreciation and amortization		
Net property, plant and equipment	11,528	7,530
	29,079	18,977
Other Assets (note A)	373	668
Total Assets	$95,298	$75,909

Cash and Marketable Securities

These two accounts, shown separately for R.E.C., Inc., are often combined as "cash and cash equivalents." The cash account is exactly that, cash in any form—cash awaiting deposit or in a bank account. Marketable securities are cash substitutes, cash that is not needed immediately in the business and is temporarily invested to earn a return. These investments are in instruments with short-term maturities (less than one year) to minimize the risk of interest-rate fluctuations. They must be relatively riskless securities and highly liquid so that funds can be readily withdrawn as needed. Instruments used for such purposes include U.S. Treasury bills, certificates, notes, and bonds; negotiable certificates of deposit at financial institutions; and commercial paper (unsecured promissory notes of large business firms). Other types of investments are listed in the noncurrent asset section of the balance sheet. Marketable securities are carried on the balance sheet at the lower of cost or market value, and the basis of measurement must be disclosed on the face of the financial statements or in notes. R.E.C., Inc. discloses the valuation in note A: "Cost approximates market value." (Notes to R.E.C., Inc. financial statements are shown on pages 7 and 8.)

Accounts Receivable

Accounts receivable are customer balances outstanding on credit sales. They are shown net of an allowance for doubtful accounts. Management estimates the dollar amount of accounts they expect will be uncollectible during an accounting period. This estimate is based on past experience, knowledge of customer quality, the state of the economy, the firm's collection policies, and other factors. Actual losses are written off against the allowance account, which is adjusted at the end of each accounting period.

The allowance for doubtful accounts can be important in assessing earnings

Inventories as a Percentage of Total Assets   **Exhibit 2.3**

Manufacturing
Drugs and Medicine	30.3
Household Electric Appliances	37.4
Sporting and Athletic Goods	40.5
Wood Furniture	33.8

Wholesale
Drugs	41.4
Electrical Appliances	49.4
Sporting Goods and Toys	50.8
Furniture	35.0

Retail
Drugs	53.0
Household Appliances	53.2
Sporting Goods and Bicycles	64.1
Furniture	49.8

Source: Robert Morris Associates, *Annual Statement Studies*, 1982.

quality. If, for instance, a company expands sales by lowering its credit standards, there should be a corresponding percentage increase in the allowance account. The estimation of this account will affect both the valuation of accounts receivable on the balance sheet and the recognition of bad debt expense on the income statement. The analyst should be alert to any change in the allowance account—both relative to the level of sales and the amount of accounts receivable outstanding—and to the justification for any deviations from past practices.

The allowance account for R.E.C., Inc. represents approximately 5% of total customer accounts receivable. To obtain the exact percentage figure, the amount in the allowance account must be added to the net accounts receivable balance shown on the face of the statement:

$$\frac{\text{Allowance for Doubtful Accounts}}{\text{Accounts receivable (net)} + \text{Allowance}} \qquad \overset{1983}{\frac{448}{8960 + 448}} = 4.8\% \qquad \overset{1982}{\frac{417}{8350 + 417}} = 4.8\%$$

An analysis of accounts receivable and its quality will be deferred to Chapter 5.

Inventories

Inventories are items held for sale or used in the manufacture of products that will be sold. A retail company, such as R.E.C., Inc., lists only one type of inventory on the balance sheet: merchandise inventories purchased for resale to the public. A manufacturing firm, in contrast, would carry three different classifications of inventory: raw materials, work-in-process, and finished goods. For most firms, inventories are the firm's major revenue producer.[3] Exhibit 2.3 illustrates the proportion of inventories for four industries at the manufacturing,

---

3. Service-oriented companies are an exception and generally have little or no inventory.

wholesale, and retail levels. For these industries—drugs, household appliances, sporting goods, and furniture—the percentage of inventories to total assets ranges from 30–40% at the manufacturing stage to about 50–65% for retail outlets. The balance sheet for R.E.C., Inc. reveals that inventories comprise slightly under 50% of total assets.

	1983	1982
$\dfrac{\text{Inventories}}{\text{Total Assets}}$	$\dfrac{\$47,041}{\$95,298} = 49.3\%$	$\dfrac{\$36,769}{\$75,909} = 48.4\%$

Given the relative magnitude of inventory, the accounting method chosen to value inventory and the associated measurement of cost of goods sold have a considerable impact on a company's financial position and operating results. Understanding the fundamentals of inventory accounting and the effect various methods have on a company's financial statements is essential to the financial statement user.

Inventory Accounting Methods— The Switch to LIFO
The method chosen by a company to account for inventory determines the value of inventory on the balance sheet and the amount of expense recognized for cost of goods sold on the income statement. The significance of inventory accounting is underlined by the presence of inflation and by the implications for tax payments and cash flow. Inventory valuation is based on an *assumption* regarding the flow of goods and has nothing whatsoever to do with the *actual* order in which products are sold. The cost flow assumption is made in order to *match* the cost of products sold during an accounting period to the revenue generated from the sales and to assign a dollar value to the inventory remaining for sale at the end of the accounting period.

The three cost-flow assumptions most frequently used by U.S. companies are FIFO (first-in, first-out), LIFO (last-in, first-out), and average cost. As the terms imply, the FIFO method assumes that the first units purchased are the first units sold during an accounting period; LIFO assumes that the items bought last are sold first; and the average cost method uses an average purchase price to cost the products sold. A simple example should highlight the differences in the three methods. A new company in its first year of operations purchases five products for sale in the order and at the prices shown:

Item	Purchase Price
#1	$5
#2	$7
#3	$8
#4	$9
#5	$11

The company sells three of these items, all at the end of the year. The cost flow assumptions would be:

Accounting Method	Goods Sold	Goods Remaining in Inventory
FIFO	#1, #2, #3	#4, #5
LIFO	#5, #4, #3	#2, #1
Average Cost	$\left(\dfrac{\text{Total Cost}}{5}\right) \times 3$	$\left(\dfrac{\text{Total Cost}}{5}\right) \times 2$

The resulting effect on the income statement and balance sheet would be:

Accounting Method	Cost of Goods Sold on Income Statement	Inventory Valuation on Balance Sheet
FIFO	$20	$20
LIFO	$28	$12
Average Cost	$24	$16

It can be clearly seen that during a period of inflation, with product prices increasing, the LIFO method produces the highest cost of goods sold expense ($28) and the lowest ending valuation of inventory ($12). Further, cost of goods sold under the LIFO method most closely approximates the current cost of inventory items since they are the most recent purchases; on the other hand, inventories on the balance sheet are undervalued with respect to replacement cost because they reflect the older costs when prices were lower. If a firm uses the LIFO method to cost inventory, there is no restatement required to adjust cost of goods sold for inflation because LIFO matches current costs to current sales. Inventory, however, would have to be revalued upward to account for inflation. FIFO has the opposite effect; during a period of rising prices, balance sheet inventory is valued at current cost, but cost of goods sold on the income statement is understated.

Accounting Trends and Techniques conducts an annual survey of the accounting practices followed by 600 industrial and merchandising corporations in the U.S. In 1970, 146 of the companies surveyed reported use of the LIFO method to account for part or all of inventory. By 1980 this number had increased to 396.[4]

Why have so many companies switched to LIFO? The answer is quite simple: taxes. Refer back to the example and note that LIFO, in a period of inflation, produces the largest cost of goods sold expense. The greater the expense deduction, the lower is taxable income. Use of LIFO reduces a company's tax bill. Unlike the case for many accounting rules (where companies are allowed to use one method for tax and another method for reporting purposes), a company that elects LIFO to figure taxable income must also use LIFO for reported income. The many companies that have switched to LIFO from other methods are apparently willing to trade lower reported earnings for the positive cash benefits resulting from LIFO's beneficial tax effect.

---

4. American Institute of Certified Public Accountants, *Accounting Trends and Techniques, 1971* and *1982*.

So far, we have seen that use of LIFO produces lower earnings than FIFO or average cost. There can be exceptions. Obviously, in a period of deflation, the results would reverse. Or firms might experience price movements that are counter to the general trend—the high technology industry, where prices on many products have declined, is a case in point. LIFO companies can also increase earnings when they sell more goods than they purchase during an accounting period, as revealed in a continuation of the inventory example.

In the example used earlier in this section, the valuation of inventory at the end of year 1 was figured as follows:

Accounting Method	Items	Inventory Valuation
FIFO	#4, #5	$20
LIFO	#1, #2	$12
Average Cost	$\left(\dfrac{\text{Total Cost}}{5}\right) \times 2$	$16

Suppose that during its second year of operations the company bought two more items:

Items	Inventory Valuation
#6	$12
#7	$14

and sold those plus the two items remaining in stock at the end of year 1. Cost of goods sold under the three assumptions would be:

Accounting Method	Old + New Inventory	Cost of Goods Sold
FIFO	$20 + $26	$46
LIFO	$12 + $26	$38
Average Cost	$16 + $26	$42

In this situation the *lowest* cost of goods sold expense results from using LIFO because the older, less expensive items were sold. Usually companies maintain a base layer of LIFO inventory that remains fairly constant. Goods are bought during the year and sales are made from the more recent purchases (for purposes of cost allocation). It is only when stocks of inventory are substantially reduced that the base layer is affected, and LIFO earnings are higher.

This very phenomenon occurred for many LIFO companies in the early 1980s when a combination of high interest rates and slow sales encouraged companies to decrease inventory levels. Two of the companies that increased earnings in 1980 and 1981 as the result of LIFO liquidation were Texaco and General Motors. Bear in mind that there is an actual reduction of inventory levels, but the earnings boost stems from the cost-flow assumption: that the older and lower priced products are those being sold. The effects can be substantial. In 1981, Texaco's earnings increased by $454 million as the direct result of partially liquidating LIFO inventory stocks; without this component added to income, Texaco's earnings would have declined between 1980 and

1981.[5] General Motors reported net income of $320 million in 1981; of this amount, $89 million came from LIFO liquidation.[6]

Because the inventory cost-flow assumption has a significant impact on financial statements, it is important to know where to find its disclosure. The method used to value inventory will be shown either on the face of the balance sheet with the inventory amount or, more commonly, in the first note to the financial statements. R.E.C., Inc. has the following explanation in note A: "Inventories are carried at the lower of cost (LIFO) or market." This statement indicates that the LIFO method is used to determine "cost." The fact that inventories are valued at the lower of cost or market reflects the accounting convention of conservatism. If the actual market value of inventory dips below "cost," as determined by the cost flow assumption (LIFO for R.E.C., Inc.), then inventory will be written down to market price. Notice that the phrase is "lower" of cost or market; the carrying amount of inventory would never be written up to market value, only down.

The note for R.E.C., Inc. (page 7) also provides information regarding the value of inventory had the FIFO method been used, since the FIFO valuation would be higher than that recorded on the balance sheet and more closely approximates current value. "If the first-in, first-out (FIFO) method of inventory accounting had been used, inventories would have been approximately $2,681,000 and $2,096,000 higher than reported at December 31, 1983 and 1982."

Prepaid Expenses

Certain expenses, such as insurance, rent, or utilities are occasionally paid in advance. They are included in current assets if they will expire within a year or an operating cycle, whichever is longer. Generally, prepayments are not material to the balance sheet as a whole. For R.E.C., Inc. prepaid expenses represent less than 1% of total current assets in 1983.

Property, Plant and Equipment

This category encompasses a company's fixed assets (also called tangible, long-lived, or capital assets), those assets not "used up" in the ebb and flow of annual business operations. These assets produce economic benefits for more than one year, and they are considered to be "tangible" because they have physical substance. Fixed assets other than land (which has a theoretically

---

5. "During 1981, worldwide inventories accounted for on the LIFO basis were partially liquidated, resulting in inventory costs prevailing in prior years, which were lower than current year's costs, being charged to 1981 cost of sales. These lower costs increased 1981 net income by approximately $454 million, after applicable income taxes." (Notes to Consolidated Financial Statements, *Texaco, Inc. 1981 Annual Report*)

6. "As a result of decreases in unit sales in 1981 and 1980, certain LIFO inventory quantities carried at lower costs prevailing in prior years as compared with the costs of current purchases were liquidated. The effect of these inventory reductions was to favorably affect income (loss) before income taxes by approximately $89.2 million and $259.2 million, respectively." (Notes to Financial Statements, *General Motors Annual Report 1981*)

unlimited life span) are "depreciated" over the period of time they benefit the firm. The process of depreciation is a method of allocating the cost of long-lived assets. The original cost, less any estimated residual value at the end of the asset's useful life, is spread over the expected life of the asset.[7] On any balance sheet date Property, Plant, and Equipment is shown at Net Book Value, which is the difference between original cost and any accumulated depreciation to date.

As discussed in Chapter 1, management has considerable discretion with respect to the depreciation of fixed assets. Depreciation involves an estimate of the economic period served by the asset and any salvage value available at the end of that period. Further, the amount of depreciation expense recognized each period is determined by the depreciation method chosen. While the total amount is the same regardless of method, the rate of cost allocation is variable. The straight line method spreads the expense evenly by periods, and the accelerated methods yield higher depreciation expense in the early years of an asset's service life. Another depreciation choice is the units-of-production method, which bases depreciation expense in a given period on actual usage. The vast majority of companies surveyed by *Accounting Trends and Techniques*[8] use the straight line method for financial reporting. In 1980, the number of companies using each method was as follows:

Straight Line	562
Accelerated	150
Units-of-Production	51

Refer now to the Property, Plant, and Equipment section of R.E.C., Inc.'s balance sheet. First note that there are three categories listed separately: land, buildings and leasehold improvements, and equipment. *Land,* as designated in the fixed asset section, refers to property used in the business; this would be land on which there are corporate offices and retail stores. Any land held for investment purposes would be segregated from property used in the business. (For R.E.C., Inc., see "Other Assets.")

R.E.C., Inc. owns some of its retail outlets, while others are leased. *Buildings* would include those stores owned by the company as well as its corporate offices. *Leasehold improvements* are additions or improvements made to leased structures. Because leasehold improvements revert to the property owner when the lease term expires, they are amortized by the lessee over the economic life of the improvement or the life of the lease, whichever is shorter.[9] *Equipment* represents the original cost, including delivery and installation charges, of the

---

7. Cost also includes any expenditures made to ready the asset for operating use.

8. American Institute of Certified Public Accountants, *Accounting Trends and Techniques,* 1982.

9. The term "amortization" is used to designate the cost allocation process for assets other than buildings, machinery, and equipment.

Net Fixed Assets as a Percentage of Total Assets   Exhibit 2.4

	%
Manufacturing	
Drugs and Medicine	24.8
Household Electric Appliances	20.9
Sporting and Athletic Goods	20.1
Wood Furniture	27.9
Wholesale	
Drugs	12.2
Electrical Appliances	8.2
Sporting Goods and Toys	9.9
Furniture	13.2
Retail	
Drugs	17.6
Household Appliances	14.5
Sporting Goods and Bicycles	14.8
Furniture	14.5

Source: Robert Morris Associates, *Annual Statement Studies*, 1982.

machinery and equipment used in business operations. Included are a variety of items such as the centralized computer system; equipment and furnishings for offices, stores, and warehouses; and delivery trucks. The final two lines under the Property, Plant, and Equipment section for R.E.C., Inc. show the amount of accumulated depreciation and amortization (for all items except land) and the amount of net property, plant, and equipment after the deduction of accumulated depreciation and amortization.

The relative proportion of fixed assets in a company's capital structure will be largely determined by the nature of the business. A firm that manufactures products would likely be more heavily invested in capital equipment than a retailer or wholesaler. Exhibit 2.4 shows the relative percentage of net fixed assets to total assets for the same four industries identified in Exhibit 2.3. As would be expected, fixed assets are most prominent at the manufacturing level; retailers are next, probably because of the need for stores and buildings in which to sell products; and the wholesale segment requires the smallest investment in fixed assets among the industries shown.

For R.E.C., Inc. net fixed assets have increased between 1983 and 1982 from 25% to 30% of total assets:

$$\frac{\text{Net property, plant, and equipment}}{\text{Total assets}} \quad \frac{\$29,079}{\$95,298} = 30.5\% \quad \frac{\$18,977}{\$75,909} = 25.0\%$$

In Chapter 5 we will develop financial ratios to measure the efficiency with which those assets are managed.

Other Assets

Other assets can include a multitude of other noncurrent items such as property held for sale, start-up costs in connection with new businesses, the cash surrender value of life insurance policies, and long-term advance payments. For R.E.C., Inc., other assets represent minor investments in property not used in business operations (explained in note A to the financial statements).

Additional categories of noncurrent assets frequently encountered (but not appearing in the R.E.C., Inc. balance sheet) are investments in the common stock of unconsolidated subsidiaries and intangible assets such as goodwill recognized in business combinations, patents, trademarks, copyrights, brand names, and franchises.

LIABILITIES

Current Liabilities

Accounts Payable

Liabilities represent claims against assets, and current liabilities are those that must be satisfied in one year or one operating cycle, whichever is longer. *Accounts payable* are short-term obligations that arise from credit extended by suppliers for the purchase of goods and services. For example, when R.E.C., Inc. buys products on credit from a wholesaler for eventual sale to its own customers, the transaction creates an account payable. This account is eliminated when the bill is paid. The ongoing process of operating the business results in the spontaneous generation of accounts payable, which increase and decrease depending on the credit policies available to the firm from its suppliers, economic conditions, and the cyclical nature of the firm's own business. Note that R.E.C., Inc. has almost doubled the amount of accounts payable between 1982 ($7,591) and 1983 ($14,294). Part of the balance sheet analysis should include an exploration of the causes for such an increase. To jump briefly ahead, the reader might also note that the income statement reveals a significant sales increase in 1983. Perhaps the rise in accounts payable is, in part, a result of this sales growth.

Notes Payable

Notes payable are short-term obligations in the form of promissory notes to suppliers or financial institutions. For R.E.C., Inc. (see note B), these are payable to a bank and reflect the amount extended under a line of credit.[10] The total amount that can be borrowed under the line of credit, according to note B, is $10,000,000. As of the end of 1983, R.E.C., Inc. had borrowed a little over half ($5,614,000) of the available amount.

Current Maturities of Long-Term Debt

When a firm has bonds, mortgages, or other forms of long-term debt outstanding, the portion of the principal that will be repaid during the upcoming year is classified as a current liability. The currently maturing debt for R.E.C., Inc. occurs as the result of several long-term obligations described in note C to the financial statements. The note lists the total amount of long-term debt outstanding, less the portion due currently, and also provides the schedule of current maturities for the next five years.

Accrued Liabilities

Like most large corporations, R.E.C., Inc. uses the accrual rather than the cash basis of accounting: revenue is recognized when it is earned, and expenses are recorded when they are incurred, regardless of when the cash is received or paid. Accrued liabilities result from the recognition of an expense in the ac-

---

10. A line of credit permits borrowing up to a maximum amount.

R.E.C., Inc. Exhibit 2.5
Consolidated Balance Sheets at December 31, 1983 and 1982
(In thousands)

	1983	1982
Liabilities and Stockholders' Equity		
Current Liabilites		
Accounts payable	$14,294	$7,591
Notes payable—banks (note B)	5,614	6,012
Current maturities of long-term debt (note C)	1,884	1,516
Accrued liabilities	5,669	5,313
Total current liabilities	27,461	20,432
Deferred Federal Income Taxes (notes A and D)	843	635
Long-Term Debt (note C)	21,059	16,975
Total liabilities	49,363	38,042
Stockholders' Equity		
Common stock, par value $1, authorized, 10,000,000 shares; issued,		
4,803,000 shares in 1983 and 4,594,000 shares in 1982 (note F)	4,803	4,594
Additional paid-in capital	957	910
Retained earnings	40,175	32,363
Total stockholders' equity	45,935	37,867
Total Liabilities and Stockholders' Equity	$95,298	$75,909

The accompanying notes are an integral part of these statements.

counting records prior to the actual payment of cash. Thus, they are liabilities because there will be an eventual cash outflow to satisfy the obligation.

Assume that a company has a $100,000 note outstanding, with 12% annual interest due in semiannual installments on March 31 and September 30. For a balance sheet prepared on December 31, interest will be accrued for three months (October, November, and December):

1. $100,000 \times .12 = $12,000$ annual interest

2. $\dfrac{\$12,000}{12} = \$1,000$ monthly interest

3. $\$1,000 \times 3 = \$3,000$ accrued interest for three months

The December 31 balance sheet would include an accrued interest liability of $3,000. Accruals also result from salaries, rent, insurance, taxes, and other expenses.

Deferred Federal Income Taxes

Deferred taxes are the product of timing differences in the recognition of revenue and expense for taxable income relative to reported income. Many companies keep two sets of books: one for the I.R.S. and one for the general public. The objective is to take advantage of all available tax deferrals in order to reduce tax payments, while showing the highest possible amount of reported net income. There are many areas in which firms are permitted to use different rules for tax and reporting purposes. A depreciation example was provided in

Chapter 1 (see page 23). Most firms use an accelerated method[11] to figure taxable income and the straight-line method for reporting purposes. The effect is to recognize more depreciation expense in the early years of an asset's useful life for tax calculations.

While depreciation methods are the most common source, other timing differences arise from the methods used to account for installment sales, long-term contracts, leases, warranties and service contracts, pensions and other employee benefits, and subsidiary investment earnings. They are called timing differences because, in theory, the total amount of expense and revenue recognized will eventually be the same for tax and reporting purposes. The deferred tax account reconciles the timing difference for any accounting period.

Assume that a company has a total annual revenue of $500,000; expenses other than depreciation are $250,000; depreciation expense is $100,000 for tax accounting and $50,000 for financial reporting (eventually this difference would reverse, and the reported depreciation expense in later years would be greater than the tax depreciation expense). Income would be computed two ways, assuming a 40% tax rate:

	Tax	Reporting
Revenue	$500,000	$500,000
Expenses	(350,000)	(300,000)
Earnings before tax	$150,000	$200,000
Tax Expense (.4)	(60,000)	(80,000)
Net Income	$ 90,000	$120,000

Taxes actually paid ($60,000) are less than tax expense ($80,000) reported in the financial statements. To reconcile the $20,000 difference between the expense recorded and the cash outflow, there is a deferred tax liability of $20,000.[12]

Tax expense (reported)	$80,000
Cash paid for taxes	(60,000)
Deferred tax liability	$20,000

Companies that invest heavily in plant and equipment are able to continue to defer taxes and thereby build the deferred tax liability account over time because, for tax purposes, accelerated depreciation is used for the newly purchased assets. In reality, the deferred tax account does not disappear because new layers of fixed assets are added, creating new and larger timing differences. The analyst is confronted with the issue of whether or not "deferred tax liablity" is a legitimate liability that represents a claim against assets. While a

---

11. The Accelerated Cost Recovery System (ACRS), specified in the Economic Recovery Tax Act of 1981.

12. If the reported tax expense were *less* than the cash paid, there would be a deferred tax charge carried in the asset section of the balance sheet.

discussion of this issue is beyond the scope of this book, it is a matter of considerable interest to the preparers and users of financial statements.[13]

Long-Term Debt

Obligations with maturities beyond one year are designated on the balance sheet as noncurrent liabilities. This category can include bonded indebtedness, long-term notes payable, mortgages, obligations under leases, pension liabilities, and long-term warranties. In note C (pages 7 and 8) to the financial statements, R.E.C., Inc. specifies the nature, maturity, and interest rate of each long-term obligation.

STOCKHOLDERS' EQUITY

The ownership interests in the company are represented in the final section of the balance sheet, stockholders' equity. Ownership equity is the residual interest in assets that remains after deducting liabilities. The owners bear the greatest risk because their claims are subordinate to creditors in the event of liquidation; but owners also benefit from the rewards of a successful enterprise. The relationship between the amount of debt and equity in a firm's capital structure and the concept of financial leverage, by which shareholder returns are magnified, will be explored in Chapter 5.

Common Stock

R.E.C., Inc. has only common stock shares outstanding. Some companies also issue preferred stock, which usually carries a fixed annual dividend payment but no voting rights. Common shareholders do not ordinarily receive a fixed return but do enjoy voting privileges in proportion to ownership interest. (Common stock dividends are declared at the discretion of a company's board of directors.) Further, common shareholders can benefit through potential share price appreciation.

The amount listed under the common stock account is based on the par or stated value of the shares issued. The par or stated value usually bears no relationship to actual market price but rather is a floor price below which the stock cannot be sold initially. At year-end 1983, R.E.C., Inc. had 4,803,000 shares outstanding of $1 par value stock, rendering a total of $4,803,000 in the common stock account.

Additional Paid-In Capital

This account reflects the amount by which the original sales price of the stock shares exceeded par value. If, for example, a company sold 1,000 shares of $1 par value stock for $3 per share, the common stock account would be $1,000, and additional paid-in capital would total $2,000.

Reference to the additional paid-in capital account for R.E.C., Inc., reveals that the firm's common stock initially sold at a price slightly higher than $1 par value. The additional paid-in capital account is not affected by the price changes resulting from stock trading subsequent to its original issue.

---

13. For additional reading on this topic, see P. Rosenfield and W. C. Dent, "No More Deferred Taxes," *Journal of Accountancy*, February, 1983.

Retained Earnings The retained earnings account is the sum of every dollar a company has earned since its inception, less any payments made to shareholders in the form of cash or stock divdends. Retained earnings do not represent a pile of unused cash stashed away in corporate vaults; instead, they are funds a company has elected to plow back into the operations of the business rather than pay out to stockholders in dividends. Retained earnings should not be confused with cash or other financial resources currently or prospectively available to satisfy financial obligations. Rather, the retained earnings account is the measurement of all undistributed earnings.

CONCLUSION Corporate balance sheets are not limited to the accounts described for R.E.C., Inc. The peruser of annual reports will encounter some additional accounts and will also confront many of the same accounts listed under a variety of other titles. Those discussed in this chapter, however, should be generally sufficient for understanding the basics of most balance sheet presentations in a set of published financial statements. The balance sheet will recur frequently through the remaining chapters of this book due to the interrelationship among the financial statements and also because of its prominent role in the analysis of financial data.

SELF-TEST Solutions are provided in Appendix D.

_____ 1. What does the balance sheet summarize for a business enterprise?
 (a) Operating results for a period.
 (b) Financial position at a point in time.
 (c) Financing and investment activities for a period.
 (d) Profit or loss at a point in time.

_____ 2. What is the balancing equation for the balance sheet?
 (a) Assets = Liabilities + Stockholders' Equity
 (b) Assets + Stockholders' Equity = Liabilities
 (c) Assets + Liabilities = Stockholders' Equity
 (d) Revenues − Expenses = Net Income

_____ 3. Why do annual reports include more than one year of the balance sheet and statements of income and changes in financial position?
 (a) It is required by law.
 (b) Financial statements for only one year would have no reference point for determining changes in a company's financial record over time.
 (c) The income statement is for a period of time, while the balance sheet is for a particular date.
 (d) The information is required as part of an intergrated disclosure system adopted by shareholders.

4. What does the cash account include? _____
   (a) Cash awaiting deposit.
   (b) Cash in bank accounts.
   (c) Both (a) and (b).
   (d) None of the above.

5. Which of the following securities would be classified as marketable secu- _____
   rities in the current asset section of the balance sheet?
   (a) Commercial paper, U.S. Treasury bills, land held for investment.
   (b) Commercial paper, U.S. Treasury bills, negotiable certificates of de-
       posit.
   (c) Commercial paper, land held for investment, bonds with maturities in
       ten years.
   (d) U.S. Treasury bills, long-term stock investment, bonds with maturities
       in ten years.

6. What type of firm generally has the highest proportion of inventory to total _____
   assets?
   (a) Retailers.
   (b) Wholesalers.
   (c) Manufacturers.
   (d) Service-oriented firms.

7. Why is the method of valuing inventory important? _____
   (a) Inventory valuation is based on the actual flow of goods.
   (b) Inventories always account for over 50% of total assets and therefore
       have a considerable impact on a company's financial position.
   (c) Companies desire to use the inventory valuation method which mini-
       mizes the cost of goods sold expense.
   (d) The inventory valuation method chosen determines the value of inven-
       tory on the balance sheet and the cost of goods sold expense on the
       income statement, two items having considerable impact on the finan-
       cial position of a company.

8. What are the three major cost-flow assumptions used by U.S. companies _____
   in valuing inventory?
   (a) LIFO, FIFO, average market.
   (b) LIFO, FIFO, actual flow.
   (c) LIFO, FIFO, average cost.
   (d) LIFO, FIFO, double-declining balance.

9. Assuming a period of inflation, which statement is true? _____
   (a) The FIFO method understates balance sheet inventory.
   (b) The FIFO method understates cost of goods sold on the income state-
       ment.
   (c) The LIFO method overstates balance sheet inventory.
   (d) The LIFO method understates cost of goods sold on the income state-
       ment.

_____ 10. Why would a company switch to the LIFO method of inventory valuation?
(a) By switching to LIFO, reported earnings will be higher.
(b) A new tax law requires companies using LIFO for reporting purposes also to use LIFO for figuring taxable income.
(c) LIFO produces the largest cost of goods sold expense in a period of inflation and thereby lowers taxable income and taxes.
(d) A survey by _Accounting Trends and Techniques_ revealed that the switch to LIFO is a current accounting "fad."

_____ 11. Where can one most typically find the cost-flow assumption used for inventory valuation for a specific company?
(a) In Robert Morris Associates, _Annual Statement Studies_.
(b) In the statement of retained earnings.
(c) On the face of the balance sheet with the total current asset amount.
(d) In the notes to the financial statements.

_____ 12. What type of firm generally has the highest proportion of fixed assets to total assets?
(a) Manufacturers.
(b) Retailers.
(c) Wholesalers.
(d) Retailers and wholesalers.

_____ 13. Companies A, B, and C:

	A	B	C
Inventory	$ 90,000	$120,000	$180,000
Property, Plant and Equipment	$ 75,000	$ 30,000	$ 45,000
Total Assets	$300,000	$300,000	$300,000

Which company is most likely a retailer? a wholesaler? a manufacturer?

(a) Company A, retailer; Company B, wholesaler; Company C manufacturer.
(b) Company A, wholesaler; Company B, manufacturer; Company C, retailer.
(c) Company A, manufacturer; Company B, wholesaler; Company C, retailer.
(d) Company A, manufacturer; Company B, retailer; Company C, wholesaler.

_____ 14. Which group of items would most likely be included in the account "Other Assets" on the balance sheet?

(a) Inventories, marketable securities, bonds.
(b) Land held for investment purposes, start-up costs, long-term prepayments.
(c) One-year prepaid insurance policy, stock investments, copyrights.
(d) Inventories, franchises, patents.

15. What do current liabilities and current assets have in common?   _____

   (a) Current assets are claims against current liabilities.
   (b) If current assets increase, then there will be a corresponding increase in current liabilities.
   (c) Current liabilities and current assets are converted into cash.
   (d) Current liabilities and current assets are those items that will be satisfied and converted into cash, respectively, in one year or one operating cycle, whichever is longer.

16. What is the difference between notes payable—banks and current maturities of long-term debt?   _____

   (a) Notes payable—banks are short-term obligations, while current maturities of long-term debt are the portion of long-term debt that will be repaid during the upcoming year.
   (b) There is no difference.
   (c) Notes payable—banks are usually included under current liabilities, and current maturities of long-term debt are included under long-term debt.
   (d) Notes payable—banks are long-term liabilities, and current maturities of long-term debt are current liabilities.

17. Which of the following items could cause the recognition of accrued liabilities?   _____

   (a) Sales, interest expense, rent.
   (b) Sales, taxes, interest income.
   (c) Salaries, rent, insurance.
   (d) Salaries, interest expense, interest income.

18. Which statement is false?   _____

   (a) Deferred taxes are the product of timing differences in the recognition of revenue and expense for taxable income relative to reported income.
   (b) Deferred taxes arise from the use of an accelerated method of depreciation for tax and reporting purposes.
   (c) Deferred taxes arise when taxes actually paid are less than tax expense reported in the financial statements.
   (d) Timing differences causing the recognition of deferred taxes may arise from the methods used to account for items such as depreciation, installment sales, leases, and pensions.

19. Which of the following would be classified as long-term debt?   _____

   (a) Mortgages, current maturities of long-term debt, bonds.
   (b) Mortgages, long-term notes payable, bonds due in ten years.
   (c) Accounts payable, bonds, obligations under leases.
   (d) Accounts payable, long-term notes payable, long-term warranties.

_____ 20. What accounts are most likely to be found in the stockholders' equity section of the balance sheet?

(a) Common stock, long-term debt, preferred stock.
(b) Common stock, additional paid-in capital, liabilities.
(c) Common stock, retained earnings, dividends payable.
(d) Common stock, additional paid-in capital, retained earnings.

_____ 21. What does the additional paid-in capital account represent?

(a) The difference between the par and the stated value of common stock.
(b) The price changes that result for stock trading subsequent to its original issue.
(c) The market price of all common stock issued.
(d) The amount by which the original sales price of stock exceeds the par value.

_____ 22. What does the retained earnings account measure?

(a) Cash held by the company since its inception.
(b) Payments made to shareholders in the form of cash or stock dividends.
(c) All undistributed earnings.
(d) Financial resources currently available to satisfy financial obligations.

23. Listed below are balance sheet accounts for Elf's Gift Shop. Mark current accounts with "C" and noncurrent accounts with "NC."

_____ (a) Long-term debt
_____ (b) Inventories
_____ (c) Accounts payable
_____ (d) Prepaid expenses
_____ (e) Equipment
_____ (f) Accrued liabilities
_____ (g) Accounts receivable
_____ (h) Cash
_____ (i) Bonds payable
_____ (j) Patents

24. Dot's Delicious Donuts has the following accounts on its balance sheet:

(1) Current assets
(2) Property, plant, and equipment
(3) Intangible assets
(4) Other assets
(5) Current liabilities
(6) Deferred Federal Income Taxes
(7) Long-term debt
(8) Stockholders' equity

How would each of the following items be classified?

(a) Land held for speculation   _____
(b) Current maturities on mortgage   _____
(c) Common stock   _____
(d) Mortgage payable   _____
(e) Balances outstanding on credit sales to customers   _____
(f) Accumulated depreciation   _____
(g) Buildings used in business   _____
(h) Accrued payroll   _____
(i) Preferred stock   _____
(j) Debt outstanding from credit extended by suppliers   _____
(k) Patents   _____
(l) Land on which warehouse is located   _____
(m) Allowance for doubtful accounts   _____
(n) Liability due to difference in taxes paid and taxes reported   _____
(o) Additional paid-in capital   _____

25. Match the following terms to the correct definitions.

(a) Consolidated financial statements	(1) Used up within one year or operating cycle, whichever is longer. _____
(b) Current	(2) Expenses incurred prior to cash outflow. _____
(c) Depreciation	(3) Value unrelated to selling price of stock. _____
(d) Deferred taxes	(4) Estimation of uncollectible accounts receivable. _____
(e) Allowance for doubtful accounts	(5) Cost allocation of fixed assets other than land. _____
(f) Prepaid expenses	(6) Expenses paid in advance. _____
(g) Current maturities	(7) Combined statements of parent company and controlled subsidiary companies. _____
(h) Accrued expense	(8) Price at which stock trades. _____
(i) Par value of stock	(9) Difference in taxes reported and taxes paid. _____
(j) Market value of stock	(10) Portion of debt to be repaid during the upcoming year. _____

The Income and 3
Retained Earnings Statements

The operating success of a business enterprise has traditionally been measured by its ability to generate earnings, the so-called "bottom line." It is hoped that the content of this book will broaden the reader's perspective of operating success to consider more than just net income or earnings per share as a yardstick. For now, however, our focus will be on the income statement and how a firm arrives at its "bottom line."

The income statement (or earnings statement) presents revenues, expenses, net income, and earnings per share for an accounting period. For published reports, the income statement is prepared for a year or a quarter. Closely related to the income statement is the statement of retained earnings. The statement of retained earnings documents the changes in the balance sheet retained earnings account from one accounting period to the next. Usually this reconciliation consists of the beginning retained earnings balance plus/minus any profit/loss for the period and less the deduction for any dividends paid. Many firms, like R.E.C., Inc., combine the presentation of the income and retained earnings statements. Both statements will be considered in this chapter, using the R.E.C., Inc. Consolidated Statements of Earnings and Retained Earnings as the basis for a description of each statement and the accounts that typically appear in the statements.

THE INCOME STATEMENT

There is no argument that the income statement is an essential ingredient in financial statement presentations and analyses, regardless of the perspective of the financial statement user—investor, creditor, employee, competitor, supplier, regulator, or other. Still, it is necessary to temper one's reliance on the income statement with the awareness that net income is not a complete and sufficient barometer of business health or financial success. The analyst must recognize that the income statement is partially the product of a wide range of accounting choices, estimates, and judgments that affect reported results, just as business policies, economic conditions, and many other variables affect reported results. The issue of potential management manipulation of earnings was considered in Chapter 1 and will be extended, where relevant, throughout this chapter. The intent is not to minimize the importance of income statement numbers but to provide a clearer context for their interpretation.

The income statement comes in two basic formats and with considerable variation in the degree of detail presented. The earnings statement for R.E.C.,

Exhibit 3.1   R.E.C., Inc.
Consolidated Statements of Earnings and Retained Earnings
For the Years ended December 31, 1983, 1982, and 1981
(In thousands except per share amounts)

	1983	1982	1981
Statements of Consolidated Earnings			
Net sales	$215,600	$153,000	$140,700
Cost of goods sold (note A)	129,364	91,879	81,606
Gross profit	86,236	61,121	59,094
Selling and administrative expenses (note A)	32,664	26,382	25,498
Advertising	14,258	10,792	9,541
Lease payments (note E)	13,058	7,111	7,267
Depreciation and amortization (note A)	3,998	2,984	2,501
Repairs and maintenance	3,015	2,046	3,031
Operating profit	19,243	11,806	11,256
Other income (expense)			
Interest income	422	838	738
Interest expense	(2,585)	(2,277)	(1,274)
Earnings before income taxes	17,080	10,367	10,720
Income taxes (notes A and D)	7,686	4,457	4,824
Net Earnings	$ 9,394	$ 5,910	$ 5,896
Earnings per common share (note G)	$1.96	$1.29	$1.33
Statements of Consolidated Retained Earnings			
Retained earnings at beginning of year	$ 32,363	$ 28,315	$ 24,260
Net earnings	9,394	5,910	5,896
Cash dividends (1983—$.33 per share; 1982 and 1981— $.41 per share)	(1,582)	(1,862)	(1,841)
Retained earnings at end of year	$ 40,175	$ 32,363	$ 28,315

The accompanying notes are an integral part of these statements.

Inc., is prepared in the *multiple-step* format, which provides several intermediate profit measures—gross profit, operating profit, and earnings before income tax—prior to the amount of net earnings for the period. The *single-step*
version of the income statement groups all items of revenue together, then
deducts all categories of expense to arrive at a figure for net income. The
Statement of Consolidated Income for Harte-Hanks Communications, Inc. and
Subsidiaries (Exhibit 3.2) illustrates the single-step approach, modified to seg-
regate the expense reported for income taxes.

Certain special items, if they occur during an accounting period, must be
disclosed separately on an income statement, regardless of format. These include the financial results of selling a major business segment, called discontinued operations; extraordinary transactions, which are defined as unusual in nature and not expected to recur in the foreseeable future[1]; and the cumulative
effect of changes in accounting principles.

---

1. Accounting Principles Board Opinion Number 30, "Reporting the Results of
Operations."

STATEMENT OF CONSOLIDATED INCOME   **Exhibit 3.2**
Harte-Hanks Communications, Inc. and Subsidiaries
Years Ended December 31, 1982, December 31, 1981 and December 31, 1980

In thousands except per share amounts	1982	1981	1980
Revenues			
Publishing advertising	$192,935	$176,415	$161,023
Publishing circulation	33,603	30,586	27,608
Publishing—other	91,815	69,455	50,849
Broadcasting and entertainment	76,004	68,354	62,436
Miscellaneous income	2,546	3,709	1,748
	396,903	348,519	303,664
Costs and Expenses			
Editorial, production and distribution	173,840	153,024	131,978
Advertising, selling, general and administrative	136,372	116,530	102,162
Depreciation and amortization (excluding goodwill)	12,276	9,853	8,156
Interest (primarily relating to long term debt)—Note B	15,931	14,302	11,986
Goodwill amortization—Note C	5,218	4,943	4,663
Miscellaneous expense	261	234	216
	343,898	298,886	259,161
Income Before Income Taxes	53,005	49,633	44,503
Income Taxes—Note F	25,708	24,271	21,806
Net Income	$ 27,297	$ 25,362	$ 22,697
Primary Earnings Per Share—Notes C and E	$2.78	$2.62	$2.38
Fully Diluted Earnings Per Share—Notes C and E	$2.66	$2.51	$2.35

See Notes to Consolidated Financial Statements

Source: Harte-Hanks Communications, Inc. 1982 Annual Report

Data are presented in corporate income statements for three years to facilitate comparison and to provide evidence regarding trends of revenues, expenses, and net earnings. The statements for R.E.C., Inc. are consolidated, which means that they are prepared on a basis that combines R.E.C., Inc. and its wholly owned subsidiaries. (The accounting methods used to account for subsidiary investments will be discussed later in this chapter under "Other Issues—Cost vs. Equity Method.")

Total sales revenue for each year of the three-year period is shown net of   **Net Sales**
returns and allowances. A sales return is a cancellation of sale, and a sales allowance is a deduction from the original sales invoice price. Since sales are the major revenue source for most companies, the trend of this figure is a key element in performance measurement. Whereas the bulk of the analytical work on R.E.C., Inc.'s financial statements will be conducted in Chapter 5, the reader should be alert to some of the obvious clues that can be gathered from a cursory walk through the income statement. It would appear, for instance, that R.E.C., Inc. had a much better sales year in 1983 than 1982. Sales grew by $62.6 million (40.9%) between 1982 and 1983, compared with $12.3 million (8.7%) between 1981 and 1982. This growth could be the result of price increases as well as a rise in the volume of products sold. The remainder of the income statement will reveal management's ability to translate sales dollars into profits.

Cost of Goods Sold The first expense deduction from sales is the cost to the seller of products sold to customers. This expense is called cost of goods sold or cost of sales. The amount of cost of goods sold for any accounting period, as explained in Chapter 2, will be affected by the cost flow assumption used to value inventory. R.E.C., Inc. uses the LIFO method, which means that the last purchases made during the year have been charged to expense. The relationship of cost of goods sold to net sales (called the cost of goods sold percentage) is an important one for profit determination because cost of goods sold is the largest expense item for most firms.

	1983	1982	1981
$\dfrac{\text{Cost of goods sold}}{\text{Net Sales}}$	$\dfrac{129,364}{215,600} = 60.0\%$	$\dfrac{91,879}{153,000} = 60.1\%$	$\dfrac{81,606}{140,700} = 58.0\%$

The cost of goods sold percentage for R.E.C., Inc. increased between 1981 and 1982. Since then, the firm has either controlled costs more effectively and/or has been able to pass along price increases to customers. The cost of goods sold percentage will vary substantially by industry, according to markup policies and other factors. For example, the cost of goods sold percentage for jewelry retailers averages 53%, compared with about 79% for retailers of groceries and meats.[2]

Gross Profit The difference between net sales and cost of goods sold is called gross profit or gross margin. Gross profit is the first step of profit measurement on the multiple-step income statement. The gross profit figure indicates how much profit the firm is generating after deducting the cost of products sold. Gross profit is frequently expressed as a percentage of net sales and is the reciprocal of the cost of goods sold percentage.

	1983	1982	1981
$\dfrac{\text{Gross profit}}{\text{Net sales}}$	$\dfrac{86,236}{215,600} = 40.0\%$	$\dfrac{61,121}{153,000} = 39.9\%$	$\dfrac{59,094}{140,700} = 42.0\%$

Operating Expense R.E.C., Inc. discloses five categories of operating expense: selling and administrative, advertising, lease payments, depreciation and amortization, and repairs and maintenance. These are all areas over which management exercises discretion and which have considerable impact on the firm's current and future profitability. Thus it is important to track these accounts carefully in terms of trends, absolute amounts, relationship to sales, and relationship to competitors.

Selling and administrative expenses are expenses relating to the sale of products or services and to the management function of the business enterprise. They include salaries, rent, insurance, utilities, supplies, and sometimes depreciation and advertising expense. R.E.C., Inc. provides separate disclosures for advertising, lease payments, and for depreciation and amortization. Note A to

---

2. Robert Morris Associates, *Annual Statement Studies,* 1981.

the R.E.C., Inc. financial statements indicates that the firm includes the expenses related to the opening of new stores in selling and administrative expense.

Advertising costs are or should be a major expense in the budgets of companies for which marketing is an important element of success. As a retail firm operating in a competitive industry, recreational products, R.E.C., Inc. spends 6 to 7 cents of every sales dollar for advertising, as indicated by the ratio of advertising to net sales:

	1983	1982	1981
Advertising / Net Sales	$\frac{14,258}{215,600} = 6.6\%$	$\frac{10,792}{153,000} = 7.1\%$	$\frac{9,541}{140,700} = 6.8\%$

Lease payments include the costs associated with operating rentals of leased facilities for retail outlets. Note E to the financial statements explains the agreements that apply to the rental arrangements and presents a schedule of minimum annual rental commitments. Observation of the sharp rise in lease payments for R.E.C., Inc. between 1982 and 1983, from $7.1 million to $13.1 million—an increase of 84%—would indicate an expansion of the firm's use of leased space.

The property leasing arrangement used by R.E.C., Inc. is known as an *operating lease,* which is a conventional rental agreement with no ownership rights transferring to the lessee at the termination of the rental contract. Another commonly used type of lease is a *capital lease.* Capital leases are, in substance, a "purchase" rather than a "lease." If a lease contract meets any one of four criteria—transfers ownership to the lessee, contains a bargain purchase option, has a lease term of 75% or more of the leased property's economic life, or has minimum lease payments with a present value of 90% or more of the property's fair value—the lease must be "capitalized" by the lessee.[3] Both the balance sheet and the income statement are affected by a capital lease. An asset and a liability are recorded on the lessee's balance sheet equal to the present value of the lease payments to be made under the contract. The asset account reflects what is, essentially, the "purchase" of an asset; and the liability is the obligation incurred in financing the "purchase." Each lease payment is apportioned partly to reduce the outstanding liability and partly to interest expense. Also, the asset account is "amortized" (amortization expense is recognized on the income statement), just as a purchased asset would be "depreciated."

Depreciation and Amortization

The cost of any asset (other than land) that will benefit a business enterprise for more than a year is allocated over the asset's service life rather than expensed in the year of purchase. Land is an exception to the rule because land is considered to have an unlimited lifespan and remains on the books at original cost. The cost allocation procedure is determined by the nature of the long-term asset. *Depreciation* is used to allocate the cost of tangible fixed assets

---

3. Statement of Financial Accounting Standards Number 13, "Accounting for Leases."

such as buildings, machinery, equipment, furniture and fixtures, and motor vehicles. *Amortization* is the process applied to the cost expiration of intangible assets: patents, copyrights, trademarks, licenses, franchises, and goodwill. The cost of acquiring and developing natural resources—oil and gas, other minerals, and standing timber—is allocated through *depletion*. The amount of expense recognized in any accounting period will depend on the level of investment in the relevant assets; estimates with regard to the asset's service life and residual value; and, for depreciation, the method used. (The reader is referred to Chapter 1 for a discussion of the financial implications of depreciation estimates and policies.)

R.E.C., Inc. recognizes annual depreciation expense for the firm's buildings and equipment and amortization expense for the leasehold improvements on rental property. Note A to the R.E.C., Inc. financial statements explains the company's procedures relating to depreciation and amortization. "Depreciation and Amortization: Property, plant, and equipment is stated at cost. Depreciation expense is calculated principally by the straight-line method based upon estimated useful lives of 3 to 10 years for equipment, 3 to 30 years for leasehold improvements, and 40 years for buildings. Estimated useful lives of leasehold improvements represent the remaining term of the lease in effect at the time the improvements are made."

The financial statement user should relate the level of property, plant, and equipment on the balance sheet to the amount of expense recognized on the income statement. For R.E.C., Inc., we would expect a fairly constant relationship between the investment in buildings, leasehold improvements, and equipment, and the annual expense recorded for depreciation and amortization:

	1983	1982
$\dfrac{\text{Depreciation and amortization}}{\text{Buildings, leasehold improvements, equipment}}$	$\dfrac{3,998}{39,796} = 10.0\%$	$\dfrac{2,984}{25,696} = 11.6\%$

The percentage of depreciation and amortization expense has decreased somewhat, possibly due to the fact that new assets were placed in service during 1983 for only part of the year, rendering less than a full year's depreciation and amortization.

In Chapter 5 we will analyze the long-run trends in these accounts by using data from earlier years, as well as the current year's financial statements.

Repairs and maintenance are the annual costs of repairing and maintaining the firm's property, plant, and equipment. Expenditures in this area should correspond to the level of investment in capital equipment and to the age and condition of the company's fixed assets. Inadequate allowance for repair and maintenance of plant and equipment can impair the ongoing operating success of a business enterprise. This category, like depreciation, should be examined in relation to the firm's investment in fixed assets:

	1983	1982
$\dfrac{\text{Repairs and maintenance}}{\text{Buildings, leasehold improvements, equipment}}$	$\dfrac{3,015}{39,796} = 7.6\%$	$\dfrac{2,046}{25,696} = 8.0\%$

Operating profit (also called EBIT, earnings before interest and taxes) is the second step of profit determination on R.E.C., Inc.'s earnings statement and measures the overall performance of the company's operations: sales revenue less the expenses associated with generating sales. The figure for operating profit provides us with a basis for assessing the success of a company apart from its financing and investment activities and separate from its tax status. The operating profit margin is calculated as the relationship between operating profit and net sales:

	1983	1982	1981
$\dfrac{\text{Operating profit}}{\text{Net sales}}$	$\dfrac{19{,}243}{215{,}600} = 8.9\%$	$\dfrac{11{,}806}{153{,}000} = 7.7\%$	$\dfrac{11{,}256}{140{,}700} = 8.0\%$

The ratio indicates that R.E.C., Inc. strengthened its return on operations in 1983, after a dip in 1982.

Other Income (Expense)

This category includes revenues and costs other than from operations: dividend and interest income, interest expense, gains (losses) from investments, and gains (losses) from the sale of fixed assets. R.E.C., Inc. recognizes as other income the interest earned on its investments in marketable securities and as other expense the interest paid on its debt. The relative amounts will be dependent upon the level of investments and the amount of debt outstanding, as well as the prevailing level of interest rates.

Earnings before income taxes is the profit recognized before the deduction of income taxes. *Income taxes* are discussed in notes to the financial statements describing the difference between the reported figure for income taxes and the actual amount of income taxes paid (see the discussion of *deferred income taxes* in Chapter 2). For R.E.C., Inc. the reader is referred to note A, which explains why the differences occur, and note D, which quantifies the reconciliation between taxes paid and tax expense reported on the income statement. R.E.C., Inc.'s average reported tax rate would be calculated by dividing income taxes on the income statement by earnings before taxes.

	1983	1982	1981
$\dfrac{\text{Income taxes}}{\text{Earnings before income taxes}}$	$\dfrac{7{,}686}{17{,}080} = 45.0\%$	$\dfrac{4{,}457}{10{,}367} = 43.0\%$	$\dfrac{4{,}824}{10{,}720} = 45.0\%$

Net earnings or "the bottom line" are the firm's profits after consideration of all revenue and expense reported during the accounting period. The net profit margin tells us the percentage of profit earned on every sales dollar:

	1983	1982	1981
$\dfrac{\text{Net earnings}}{\text{Net sales}}$	$\dfrac{9{,}394}{215{,}600} = 4.4\%$	$\dfrac{5{,}910}{153{,}000} = 3.9\%$	$\dfrac{5{,}896}{140{,}700} = 4.2\%$

In 1983 R.E.C., Inc., earned 4.4 cents on every $1 of sales, reflecting an improvement over the previous two years: 3.9 cents in 1982 and 4.2 cents in 1981. Reasons for the improvement will be explored in Chapter 5.

Earnings per common share is the net earnings for the period divided by the average number of common stock shares outstanding. This figure shows the return to the common stock shareholder for every share owned. R.E.C., Inc. earned $1.96 per share in 1983, compared with $1.29 per share in 1982 and $1.33 per share in 1981. (Note G to the financial statements lists the weighted average number of shares used to compute earnings per share for each of the three years.)

Companies with complex capital structures—which means existence of convertible securities (such as bonds convertible into common stock), stock options, and warrants—must calculate two amounts for earnings per share, *primary* and *fully diluted*. If convertible securities were converted into common stock and/or the options and warrants were exercised, there would be more shares outstanding for every dollar earned, and the potential for dilution is accounted for by the dual presentation. The dual presentation is required if the potential dilution would reduce earnings per share by 3% or more. (In note G to the financial statements R.E.C., Inc. reports that the potential for dilution is less than 3% of earnings per share and, thus, the firm reports only one earnings per share amount.) The primary earnings per share figure is based on the assumption that only some[4] of the potentially dilutive securities have been converted into common stock, while fully diluted earnings per share includes all potentially dilutive securities in the number of shares outstanding. It is important that the user of the financial data be aware of the different computation methods in order to determine what the earnings per share figures represent. The dual presentation of earnings per share for Harte-Hanks Communications, Inc. is illustrated in Exhibit 3.2, on page 57.

THE STATEMENT OF RETAINED EARNINGS

The retained earnings statement is ordinarily the shortest and least complicated of the four financial statements. The retained earnings statement details the transactions (primarily net income and dividends) that affect the balance sheet retained earnings account during an accounting period. The starting point is the retained earnings balance at the beginning of the accounting period. To that balance net earnings are added or net losses are deducted. Dividends, both cash and stock, are subtracted to arrive at the ending balance.

The statements of consolidated retained earnings for R.E.C., Inc., like the income statements, are presented for three years. The net earnings for each year have been added to the beginning balance of retained earnings. The only deduction for R.E.C., Inc. has been the annual payment of cash dividends. In 1983 R.E.C., Inc. paid cash dividends of $.33 per share on average shares outstanding (Note G) of 4,792,857 for a total of $1,581,643. The amount of the dividend payment was reduced from $.41 per share in 1982 and 1981.

---

4. Included are those securities considered to be *dilutive* common stock equivalents. Accounting Principles Board Opinion Number 15 defines common stock equivalents as securities that contain a provision that enables the owner to convert them into common stock.

Statements of Consolidated Retained Earnings   Exhibit 3.3

Retained earnings at beginning of year	$ 32,363	$ 28,315	$ 24,260
Net earnings	9,394	5,910	5,896
Cash dividends (1983—$.33 per share; 1982 and 1981—$.41 per share)	(1,582)	(1,862)	(1,841)
Retained earnings at end of year	$ 40,175	$ 32,363	$ 28,315

The accompanying notes are an integral part of these statements.

Although R.E.C., Inc. paid no stock dividends, the financial statement user should be aware of the accounting treatment of these dividends.

Stock dividends are the issuance to existing shareholders of additional shares in proportion to current ownership. When a stock dividend is declared the retained earnings account is decreased by the *market* value of the shares issued in the case of a small stock dividend (less than 20–25% of the number of shares outstanding) or by the *par* value of the stock in the case of a large stock dividend (more than 20–25% of the number of shares outstanding). For example, if a company with 100,000 ($1 par) common shares outstanding issues a 10% stock dividend at a time when the market value of the stock is $3, the retained earnings account will be reduced by $30,000:

$$(100,000 \times .10) \times \$3 = \$30,000.$$

If a 50% stock dividend were paid, the deduction would be $50,000:

$$(100,000 \times .5) \times \$1 = \$50,000.$$

From the stockholders' viewpoint, receipt of a stock dividend, unlike a cash dividend, represents nothing of tangible value. When a cash dividend is paid the shareholder receives cash, and the company's assets and retained earnings are reduced. Payment of a stock dividend does not affect assets or liabilities but results only in an adjustment within the equity section of the balance sheet: the retained earnings' balance is reduced, and the stock account (or stock and paid-in capital) is increased by the same amount. The shareholder has more shares, but the proportion of ownership in the company is exactly the same, and the net asset value (assets minus liabilities) of the company is exactly the same. The market value of the stock should drop in proportion to the additional shares issued.

Transactions other than the recognition of net profit/loss and the payment of dividends can cause changes in the retained earnings balance. These include prior period adjustments and certain changes in accounting principles. Prior period adjustments result primarily from the correction of errors made in previous accounting periods; the beginning retained earnings balance is adjusted for the year in which the error is discovered. Some changes in accounting principles, such as a change from LIFO to any other inventory method, also cause an adjustment to retained earnings for the cumulative effect of the change.

Statements of Shareholders' Equity

Some companies adopt a broader approach and prepare a statement that summarizes changes in the entire shareholders' equity section of the balance sheet, including not only retained earnings but also all of the other equity accounts. Exhibit 3.4 shows the Consolidated Statements of Shareholders' Equity for Sears, Roebuck and Co. from the 1981 annual report in dollars and shares. Note that the statement covers common stock, capital in excess of par value (which is another term used for additional paid-in capital), and retained income (retained earnings). Three additional accounts, not previously discussed, are also included: treasury stock, unrealized gains (losses) on marketable equity securities, and cumulative translation adjustments.

When a firm repurchases (but does not retire) shares of its own stock, these shares are designated as *treasury stock* and are subtracted from the total stockholders' equity section. *Unrealized gains (losses) on marketable equity securities* arise from an accounting rule that requires that investments in marketable equity securities be carried at the lower of cost or market[5]; for noncurrent securities unrealized losses (write-down of securities when market value is below cost) or unrealized gains (write-up of securities to original cost if market value recovers for a security previously written down) are disclosed in the equity section. The equity section also shows *cumulative translation adjustments,* which result from the translation of foreign currency financial statements.[6]

Other Issues— Cost vs. Equity Method

Before leaving the income and retained earnings statements, it is desirable to consider an additional issue that the financial statement user frequently encounters in attempting to understand financial statement data. The method—cost or equity—used to account for investments in the voting stock of other companies can be confusing or misleading to a novice reader. This is not a significant issue for R.E.C., Inc. because the parent owns 100% of the voting stock in its subsidiaries; R.E.C., Inc. and its subsidiaries are, in reality, one consolidated entity. The controversy over the cost vs. the equity method comes into play for stock investments of less than 50%, where consolidated financial statements are not prepared.

Accounting rules permit two different methods to account for stock investments of less than 50%. The *equity* method allows the investor proportionate recognition of the investee's net income, irrespective of the payment or nonpayment of cash dividends; under the *cost* method, the investor recognizes investment income only to the extent of any cash dividends received. At issue in the choice of accounting methods is whether the investor exercises control over the investee.

Accounting Principles Board Opinion Number 18 specifies that the equity method of accounting should be used when the investor can exercise *significant*

---

5. Statement of Financial Accounting Standards Number 12, "Accounting for Certain Marketable Securities."

6. Statement of Financial Accounting Standards Number 52, "Foreign Currency Translation."

Sears, Roebuck and Co.
Consolidated Statements of Shareholders' Equity

Exhibit 3.4

	Year Ended December 31					
	1981	1980*	1979*	1981	1980*	1979*
	millions			shares in thousands		
Preferred shares; authorized 50 million shares, $1.00 par value, none issued.						
Common shares—$.75 par value, 500 million shares authorized; issued as follows:						
Balance, beginning of year	$ 244.0	$ 243.5	$ 243.0	325,335.0	324,647.2	323,902.8
Issued for acquired companies (note 2)	24.5	—	—	32,619.3	—	—
Issued under incentive compensation plan	—	—	—	27.0	7.7	61.7
Dividends reinvested	—	.5	.5	—	680.1	682.7
Stock options exercised	—	—	—	13.9	—	—
Balance, end of year	268.5	244.0	243.5	357,995.2	325,335.0	324,647.2
Capital in excess of par value						
Balance, beginning of year	640.5	629.5	614.9			
Issued for acquired companies	508.8	—	—			
Issued under incentive compensation plan	.4	.1	1.2			
Dividends reinvested	—	11.0	13.0			
Stock options exercised and other changes	(5.8)	(.1)	.4			
Balance, end of year	1,143.9	640.5	629.5			
Retained income						
Balance, beginning of year	6,820.2	6,639.8	6,218.9			
Net income	650.1	609.8	829.5			
Dividends ($1.36, $1.36 and $1.28 per share)	(429.1)	(429.4)	(408.6)			
Balance, end of year	7,041.2	6,820.2	6,639.8			
Treasury stock (at cost)						
Balance, beginning of year	(192.4)	(142.9)	(10.5)	(10,167.6)	(7,084.6)	(508.0)
Purchased	(5.1)	(54.3)	(132.4)	(299.8)	(3,331.7)	(6,576.6)
Exchanged for Sears debt (note 8)	30.3	—	—	1,606.0	—	—
Issued to subsidiary in connection with acquisition (note 2)	(37.8)	—	—	(2,216.4)	—	—
Reissued under dividend reinvestment plan	18.3	4.8	—	970.5	248.7	—
Balance, end of year	(186.7)	(192.4)	(142.9)	(10,107.3)	(10,167.6)	(7,084.6)
Unrealized net capital gains (losses) on marketable equity securities						
Balance, beginning of year	152.4	76.0	(3.4)			
Net increase (decrease)	(103.9)	76.4	79.4			
Balance, end of year	48.5	152.4	76.0			
Cumulative translation adjustments (note 1)						
Initial application of SFAS No. 52	(29.3)					
Unrealized exchange adjustments	(17.2)					
Balance, end of year	(46.5)					
Total shareholders' equity and shares outstanding	$8,268.9	$7,664.7	$7,445.9	347,887.9	315,167.4	317,562.6

See accompanying notes which include the summarized Group related financial statements.
*Restated (see note 1, page 43).

Source: Sears, Roebuck and Co. Annual Report, 1981.

influence over the investee's operating and financing policies. No problem exists where there is ownership of 50% or more because, clearly, one company can control the other. But at what level below 50% ownership can one firm substantially influence the affairs of another firm? Although there can be exceptions, 20% ownership of voting stock is generally considered to be evidence of substantial influence. There are, however, circumstances in which less than 20% reflects control and cases in which more than 20% ownership does not. What difference does it make whether a company uses the cost or the equity method? An illustration should help provide an answer.

Assume that Company A owns exactly 20% of the voting common stock of Company B. Company B reports $100,000 of earnings for the year and elects to pay *no* cash dividends. The income recognition effect for the investor, Company A, would be entirely different depending on the accounting method used for the investment:

Cost Method	Equity Method
Investment Income $0	Investment Income $20,000

The cost method allows recognition of investment income only to the extent of any cash dividends actually received, whereas the equity method permits the investor to count as income its percentage interest in the investee's earnings.

Company B's Earnings	$100,000
Company A's % Ownership	× .20
Company A's Investment Income	$ 20,000

Use of the equity method somewhat distorts earnings in the sense that income is recognized where no cash may ever be received because it is presumed that the investor, through its control of voting shares, could cause Company B to pay cash dividends.[7] In reality this may not be true, and the investor is counting as income earnings that are not available to spend.

In Chapter 4 we will consider performance measures other than net income. One of the adjustments made to net income will be the deduction of income accrued on stock investments under the equity method of accounting.

Other Issues— Inflation and Segmental Accounting

Two additional topics, which are directly related to the income statement, are covered in Appendix B and Appendix C. The first deals with the impact of inflation on reported earnings (Appendix B, "Accounting for Inflation"). The effect of inflation on balance sheet and income measurement was introduced in Chapter 1 as one of the obstacles confronting the user of conventional financial statements. The appendix will present a discussion of the distortions caused by inflation and illustrate the supplementary disclosures required by the Financial Accounting Standards Board to account for inflation.

The second appendix (Appendix C, "The Analysis of Segmental Data") will deal with the supplementary information reported by companies that operate in different industries. Segmental data include revenue, operating profit or loss, identifiable assets, depreciation and amortization, and capital expenditures by industry component. This information permits the analysis of operating performance and contribution by each segment of the company.

---

7. The balance sheet Investment account is also affected; the account is increased by the amount investment income exceeds cash dividends received (or decreased by an investment loss) under the equity method.

Solutions are provided in Appendix D.   **SELF-TEST**

1. What does the income statement measure for a firm?   _____
   (a) The changes in assets and liabilities that occurred during the period.
   (b) The financing and investment activities for a period.
   (c) The results of operations for a period.
   (d) The financial position of a firm for a period.

2. Which two financial statements are frequently combined for presentation   _____
   purposes?
   (a) The statement of financial position and the balance sheet.
   (b) The income and retained earnings statements.
   (c) The statement of changes in financial position and the retained earn-
       ings statement.
   (d) The balance sheet and the income statement.

3. Which of the items below need *not* be disclosed separately in the income   _____
   statement?
   (a) Salary expense.
   (b) Selling a major business segment.
   (c) Extraordinary transactions.
   (d) Cumulative effect of changes in accounting principles.

4. Why are data presented in income statements for three years?   _____
   (a) The IRS requires a three-year presentation for tax purposes.
   (b) A three-year presentation discourages manipulation of earnings by
       management.
   (c) Income statements for three years facilitate comparison and provide
       evidence regarding trends of revenues, expenses, and net earnings.
   (d) An income statement for only one year would be meaningless.

5. What is the largest expense item for most firms?   _____
   (a) Gross profit.
   (b) Depreciation.
   (c) Operating expense.
   (d) Cost of goods sold.

6. What is the basic difference between an operating lease and a capital lease?   _____
   (a) A capital lease is, in substance, a purchase, whereas an operating lease
       is a rental agreement.
   (b) An operating lease transfers ownership to the lessee.
   (c) Capital leases must meet four criteria.
   (d) Capital leases must have a lease term of 90% or more of the leased
       property's economic life.

_____ 7. Which of the following statements is incorrect with regard to capital leases?
   (a) The balance sheet and the income statement are affected by a capital lease.
   (b) Each lease payment is apportioned partly to interest expense and partly to reduce a liability.
   (c) The liability account is amortized just as a purchased asset would be depreciated.
   (d) An asset and a liability are recorded on the lessee's balance sheet equal to the present value of the lease payments to be made under the contract.

_____ 8. Which of the following assets will not be depreciated over its service life?
   (a) Buildings.
   (b) Furniture.
   (c) Equipment.
   (d) Land.

_____ 9. How are costs of assets that benefit a firm for more than one year allocated?
   (a) Depreciation.
   (b) Depletion and amortization.
   (c) Costs are divided by service lives of assets and allocated to repairs and maintenance.
   (d) Both (a) and (b).

_____ 10. Why should the expenditures for repairs and maintenance correspond to the level of investment in capital equipment and to the age and condition of that equipment?
   (a) Repairs and maintenance expense is calculated in the same manner as depreciation expense.
   (b) Inadequate repairs of equipment can impair the operating success of a business enterprise.
   (c) It is a generally accepted accounting principle that repairs and maintenance expense is generally between 5% and 10% of fixed assets.
   (d) Repairs and maintenance are depreciated over the remaining life of the assets involved.

_____ 11. Why is the figure for operating profit important?
   (a) This is the figure used for calculating federal income tax expense.
   (b) The figure for operating profit provides a basis for assessing the success of a company apart from its financing and investment activities and separate from its tax status.
   (c) The operating profit figure includes all operating revenues and expenses as well as interest and taxes related to operations.
   (d) The figure for operating profit provides a basis for assessing the wealth of a firm.

12. What are three profit measures calculated from the income statement? _____
    (a) Gross profit margin, operating profit margin, net profit margin.
    (b) Gross profit, cost of goods sold percentage, EBIT.
    (c) Operating profit margin, net profit margin, repairs and maintenance to fixed assets.
    (d) None of the above.

13. When is a dual presentation of primary and fully diluted earnings per share required? _____
    (a) If the potential dilution would reduce earnings per share by 3% or more.
    (b) If convertible securities were in fact converted.
    (c) If a company has a complex capital structure.
    (d) If a company has stock options and warrants outstanding.

14. What is the impact of a stock dividend on the financial statements? _____
    (a) Cash is reduced on the balance sheet, and common stock is increased.
    (b) The proportion of ownership in the company will increase.
    (c) The retained earnings balance is reduced, and the stock account is increased by the same amount.
    (d) The retained earnings account is decreased by the par value of the shares issued in the case of a small stock dividend or by the market value in the case of a large dividend.

15. Which of the following cause a change in the retained earnings account balance? _____
    (a) Prior period adjustment.
    (b) Payment of dividends.
    (c) Net profit or loss.
    (d) All of the above.

16. What is a statement of shareholders' equity? _____
    (a) It is the same as a retained earnings statement.
    (b) It is a statement that reconciles the treasury stock account.
    (c) It is a statement that summarizes changes in the entire shareholder's equity section of the balance sheet.
    (d) It is a statement reconciling the difference between stock issued at par value and stock issued at market value.

17. What additional shareholder equity accounts can be found on a statement of shareholder's equity as compared to a statement of retained earnings? _____
    (a) Investments in other companies.
    (b) Treasury stock, unrealized gains (losses) on marketable equity securities, and cumulative translation adjustment.
    (c) Market value of treasury stock.
    (d) Both (a) and (c)

_____ 18. Why can the equity method of accounting for investments in the voting stock of other companies cause distortions in net earnings?
(a) Income is recognized where no cash may ever be received.
(b) Significant influence may exist even if the ownership of voting stock is less than 20%.
(c) Income should be recognized in accordance with the accrual method of accounting.
(d) Income is recognized only to the extent of cash dividends received.

_____ 19. Match the following terms with the correct definitions:

(a) Depreciation	(h) Cost method
(b) Depletion	(i) Single-step format
(c) Amortization	(j) Multiple-step format
(d) Gross profit	(k) Primary earnings per share
(e) Operating profit	(l) Fully diluted earnings per share
(f) Net profit	(m) Operating lease
(g) Equity method	(n) Capital lease

Definitions:

_____ 1. Proportionate recognition of investee's net income for investments in voting stock of other companies.

_____ 2. Presentation of income statement that provides several intermediate profit measures.

_____ 3. Conventional rental agreement with no ownership rights transferring to the lessee at the termination of the contract.

_____ 4. Allocation of costs of tangible fixed assets.

_____ 5. Difference between sales revenue and expenses associated with generating sales.

_____ 6. Recognition of income from investments in voting stock of other companies to the extent of cash dividend received.

_____ 7. Rental agreement which is, in substance, a purchase.

_____ 8. Difference between net sales and cost of goods sold.

_____ 9. Allocation of costs of acquiring and developing natural resources.

_____ 10. Earnings per share figure based on the assumption that some of the potentially dilutive securities have been converted to common stock.

_____ 11. Presentation of income statement that groups all revenue items, then deducts all expenses, to arrive at net income.

_____ 12. Earnings per share figure based on the assumption that all potentially dilutive securities have been converted to common stock.

_____ 13. Allocation of costs of intangible assets.

_____ 14. Difference between all revenues and expenses.

20. The following categories appear on the income statement of Joshua Jeans
    Company:
    (a) Net sales   (d) Other revenue/expense
    (b) Cost of sales   (e) Income tax expense
    (c) Operating expenses

Classify the following items according to income statement category.
    1. Depreciation expense   ——
    2. Interest revenue   ——
    3. Sales revenue   ——
    4. Advertising expense   ——
    5. Interest expense   ——
    6. Sales returns and allowances   ——
    7. Federal income taxes   ——
    8. Repairs and maintenance   ——
    9. Selling and administrative expenses   ——
    10. Cost of products sold   ——
    11. Dividend income   ——
    12. Lease payments   ——

The Statement of 4
Changes in Financial Position
and Cash Flow from Operations

In *Alice's Adventures in Wonderland,*[1] Lewis Carroll creates the following exchange between Alice and the Cheshire Cat:

> ALICE: Would you tell me please, which way I ought to walk from here?
>
> CHESHIRE CAT: That depends a good deal on where you want to get to.
>
> ALICE: I don't much care where . . .
>
> CHESHIRE CAT: Then it doesn't matter which way you walk.
>
> ALICE: . . . so long as I get *somewhere.*
>
> CHESHIRE CAT: Oh, you're sure to do that, if you only walk long enough.

Perhaps an analogy between Alice's journey and the statement of changes in financial position is somewhat implausible, but there is a relevant message in the Cheshire Cat's advice that you're sure to get somewhere if only you walk long enough. For the novice financial statement user, the statement of changes in financial condition is probably the least understood and most underutilized of the four basic financial statements. In spite of its apparent complexity, however, the statement is the most potentially beneficial single store of information in a corporate annual report. This chapter will hopefully serve as a "walk long enough" to get through the basics of what the statement is all about and how to use the information it contains, including an exploration of a critically important analytical tool, cash flow from operations. A rosy net income figure is ultimately insignificant unless a company can translate its earnings into cash; and the only place in an annual report where we can learn about the generation of cash from operations is the statement of changes in financial position.

The pattern followed in the preceding chapters on the balance sheet, earnings, and retained earnings statements will be continued in this chapter. The Consolidated Statement of Changes in Financial Position for R.E.C., Inc. will serve as the background for an account-by-account description of the statement

---

1. Lewis Carroll, *Alice's Adventures in Wonderland* (New York: Derrydale Books, 1979), pp. 89–90. Also see James C. Fenhagen, *More Than Wanderers* (New York: The Seabury Press, 1978), Chapter V.

and its implications for financial analysis. The second part of the chapter will focus on the calculation of cash flow provided by operations from the typical statement of changes format and will include a discussion of the significance of cash flow in assessing financial performance.

THE STATEMENT OF CHANGES IN FINANCIAL POSITION

The statement of changes in financial position, unofficially called "the sources and uses of funds statement," summarizes a firm's financing and investing activities for an accounting period and explains the change in financial position from one period to the next. The statement is extremely useful to the financial analyst because it provides insight into management's financial policies and strategies by disclosing a firm's sources of funds (profits from operating the business, long-term borrowing, issuance of capital stock, proceeds from sale of long-term assets) and uses of funds (outlays for purchases of fixed assets or intangibles, investments in stock, payment of cash dividends, repayment of long-term debt).

The term "funds" can mean either *cash* or *working capital*. *Cash* is the narrower interpretation of funds. A statement of changes in financial position prepared on a cash basis explains the change in the balance sheet cash account, or cash plus cash equivalents (short-term investments in marketable securities), during the accounting period. *Working capital* is the amount by which current assets exceed current liabilities and thus is a broader concept of funds covering changes in cash as well as all other current assets and all current liabilities.

Like R.E.C., Inc., most companies prepare the statement of changes in financial position on a *working capital* basis. Of the 600 companies surveyed by *Accounting Trends and Techniques* in 1980, 541 (90%) defined funds as working capital.[2] The Financial Accounting Standards Board recently issued an exposure draft, which emphasizes the cash concept.[3] The ultimate outcome may be a more widespread adoption of the cash approach and/or a new format for the statement of changes in financial position.

Regardless of how funds are defined, the statement must disclose all material aspects of the firm's financing and investment activities, including those that do not affect cash or working capital. For example, the conversion of bonds into common stock or the direct exchange of property for other property would be disclosed in the statement of changes in financial position, along with the sources and uses of cash or working capital.

Clues

To make what seems to be a complicated financial statement less of a challenge, the reader is entitled to two simple clues. First, the statement of changes in financial position is, in reality, a reformulation of the balance sheet supple-

---

2. American Institute of Certified Public Accounts, *Accounting Trends and Techniques,* 1982.

3. Financial Accounting Standards Board, Exposure Draft of Proposed Statement of Financial Accounting Concepts, "Reporting Income, Cash Flows, and Financial Position of Business Enterprises," 1981.

R.E.C., Inc. Exhibit 4.1
Consolidated Statements of Changes in Financial Position
For the years ended December 31, 1983, 1982, and 1981
(In thousands)

	1983	1982	1981
Sources of working capital			
From operations			
Net earnings for the year	$ 9,394	$ 5,910	$5,896
Charges to earnings not using working capital			
Depreciation and amortization (note A)	3,998	2,984	2,501
Deferred income taxes—noncurrent (notes A and D)	208	136	118
Working Capital provided from operations	13,600	9,030	8,515
Additions to long-term debt	5,600	7,882	629
Sales of common stock	256	183	124
Other sources	295	—	—
Total Sources	19,751	17,095	9,268
Uses of working capital			
Additions to property, plant and equipment	14,100	4,773	3,982
Reductions of long-term debt	1,516	1,593	127
Cash dividends	1,582	1,862	1,841
Total Uses	17,198	8,228	5,950
Increase in Working Capital	$ 2,553	$ 8,867	$3,318
(15) Changes in components of working capital			
Increase (decrease) in current assets			
Cash	$ 1,679	(235)	$ 782
Marketable securities	(2,732)	(1,841)	976
Accounts receivable—net	610	3,339	448
Inventories	10,272	7,006	2,331
Prepaid expenses	(247)	(295)	82
	9,582	7,974	4,619
Increase (decrease) in current liabilities			
Accounts payable	6,703	(1,051)	902
Notes payable—banks	(398)	1,931	1,452
Current maturities of long-term debt	368	(77)	(126)
Accrued liabilities	356	(1,696)	(927)
	7,029	(893)	1,301
Increase in Working Capital	$ 2,553	$ 8,867	$3,318

The accompanying notes are an integral part of these statements.

mented by detail extracted from the income statement and notes to the financial statements. What the statement of changes actually does is to explain changes in cash and cash equivalents or changes in working capital by analyzing the changes in all of the other balance sheet accounts. Since the balance sheet balances (assets = liabilities + stockholders' equity), the statement of changes in financial position must also balance (sources − uses = change in cash or working capital).

Exhibit 4.2 presents a condensed version of the R.E.C., Inc. balance sheet with a column showing the changes in account balances between year-end 1982 and 1983. (Since R.E.C., Inc. uses the working capital concept, that will be the approach used for our discussion of the statement.) The change in working

Exhibit 4.2   **R.E.C., Inc.**
Condensed Consolidated Balance Sheets at December 31, 1983 and 1982
(In thousands)

	1983	1982	$ Change
Assets			
Total current assets	$65,846	$56,264	+ 9,582
Property, Plant, and Equipment	40,607	26,507	+14,100
Less: Accumulated depreciation and amortization	(11,528)	(7,530)	+ (3,998)
Other Assets	373	668	− 295
Total Assets	$95,298	$75,909	+19,389
Liabilities and Stockholders' Equity			
Total current liabilities	$27,461	$20,432	+ 7,029
Deferred Federal Income Taxes	843	635	+ 208
Long-Term Debt	21,059	16,975	+ 4,084
Common stock	4,803	4,594	+ 209
Additional paid-in capital	957	910	+ 47
Retained earnings	40,175	32,363	+ 7,812
Total Liabilities and Stockholders' Equity	$95,298	$75,909	+19,389

capital (the increase in current assets less the increase in current liabilities) will be explained by analyzing the changes in all of the noncurrent accounts and listing them as a source or use of working capital.

The second clue is a simple rule to determine what constitutes a source of funds and what results in a use of funds when analyzing the net change in an account balance[4]:

	Source	**Use**
	− Asset	+ Asset
	+ Liability and Equity	− Liability and Equity

The table indicates that a decrease in an asset balance or an increase in liability and equity accounts are sources of funds. An example from Exhibit 4.2 would be the increase in common stock and additional paid-in capital (equity accounts); proceeds from the sale of stock provide a source of funds. On the other hand, the increase in property, plant, and equipment (asset account) is a use of funds; that is, funds have been "used" to invest in fixed assets. With any simple rule, there are complications.

Accumulated depreciation appears in the asset section but actually is a contra-asset because it reduces the net amount of total assets. Thus, accumulated depreciation is shown in parentheses in Exhibit 4.2 and has the same effect as the change in a liability account. Another complication occurs from the impact of conflicting transactions in one account. For example, the net

---

4. For a reader trained in the accounting terminology of debits and credits, a more definitive version of this illustration would be:

Source	**Use**
− Debit	+ Debit
+ Credit	− Credit

increase in retained earnings has been caused by the combined impact of net earnings, which increase the account, and dividend payments, which reduce the account; the long-term debt account increased on a net basis, but there were both reductions in and additions to long-term borrowing to account for this change. In these areas it is necessary to use income statement data and material from the financial statement notes to explain fully the changes in balance sheet accounts.[5]

Explanation of the Statement

The Consolidated Statement of Changes in Financial Position for R.E.C., Inc. is prepared on a working capital basis and thus discloses sources and uses of working capital. As with the earnings and retained earnings statements, comparative data for three years must be presented. Let us begin the explanation not at the beginning, but in the middle of the R.E.C., Inc. Consolidated Statements of Changes in Financial Position with the line "Increase in Working Capital." Each account on the R.E.C., Inc. Statements of Changes in Financial Position for 1983 (Exhibit 4.3) will be referenced to the appropriate changes (year-end 1982 to 1983) in balance sheet accounts. Numerical keys are provided to help the reader find the appropriate account on the R.E.C., Inc. Consolidated Statement of Changes in Financial Position and, where relevant, to match the account with the "change" column of Exhibit 4.4 (page 79).

(1) Increase in working capital is the balancing figure for the statement. Focusing on the year 1983, the increase in working capital of $2,553 thousand was obtained by subtracting the net change in current liability accounts for the year from the net change in current asset accounts (Exhibit 4.3):

	$ Change
Total current assets	+ 9,582
Less: Total current liabilities	(7,029)
Change in Working Capital	+ 2,553

The increase in working capital of $2,553 thousand indicates that during 1983 the sources of working capital exceeded the uses of working capital by $2,553 thousand. Had the uses been greater than the sources, there would be a decrease in working capital. The section above the increase in working capital explains the change by listing all of the sources and uses of funds. (There are a variety of formats for presenting the statement of changes in financial position; thus the change in working capital is not always found in the middle of the statement.)

(2) Sources of working capital are those transactions that cause an inflow of working capital into the firm. There are four primary sources of working capital: 1) operations, 2) long-term borrowing, 3) issuance of equity securities, and 4) disposal of noncurrent assets.

---

5. For some companies the complete detail of account transactions is available only in the firm's accounting records, and it is not possible to reconcile every account change from published data.

Exhibit 4.3 R.E.C., Inc.
Consolidated Statements of Changes in Financial Position
For the years ended December 31, 1983, 1982, and 1981
(In thousands)

	1983	1982	1981
(2) Sources of working capital			
(3) From operations			
(4) Net earnings for the year	$ 9,394	$ 5,910	$5,896
(5) Charges to earnings not using working capital			
(6) Depreciation and amortization	3,998	2,984	2,501
(note A)			
(7) Deferred income taxes—noncurrent			
(notes A and D)	208	136	118
Working Capital provided from operations	13,600	9,030	8,515
(8) Additions to long-term debt	5,600	7,882	629
(9) Sales of common stock	256	183	124
(10) Other sources	295	—	—
Total Sources	19,751	17,095	9,268
(11) Uses of working capital			
(12) Additions to property, plant and equipment	14,100	4,773	3,982
(13) Reductions of long-term debt	1,516	1,593	127
(14) Cash dividends	1,582	1,862	1,841
Total Uses	17,198	8,228	5,950
(1) Increase in Working Capital	$ 2,553	$ 8,867	$3,318
(15) Changes in components of working capital			
Increase (decrease) in current assets			
Cash	$ 1,679	$ (235)	$ 782
Marketable securities	(2,732)	(1,841)	976
Accounts receivable—net	610	3,339	448
Inventories	10,272	7,006	2,331
Prepaid expenses	(247)	(295)	82
	9,582	7,974	4,619
Increase (decrease) in current liabilities			
Accounts payable	6,703	(1,051)	902
Notes payable—banks	(398)	1,931	1,452
Current maturities of long-term debt	368	(77)	(126)
Accrued liabilities	356	(1,696)	(927)
	7,029	(893)	1,301
Increase in Working Capital	$ 2,553	$8,867	$3,318

The accompanying notes are an integral part of these statements.

(3) From operations. The statements of changes in financial position for each period begin with funds provided by operations. These are the funds generated "internally," through the firm's normal business activities. The starting point for determining working capital from operations is **(4)** net earnings for the period from the income statement ($9,394 thousand for R.E.C., Inc. in 1983). This figure is then adjusted for **(5)** items recognized in determining net income but which did not use or provide working capital. Sounds complicated? It is somewhat, but the adjustment also makes sense.

Consider depreciation. Depreciation expense is deducted on the income statement to determine net income. But remember that depreciation is the allocation of a cost and does not require any outflow of funds in the current year.

Condensed Consolidated Balance Sheets at December 31, 1983, and 1982   **Exhibit 4.4**
(In thousands)

	1983	1982	$ Change	
Assets				
Total current assets	$65,846	$56,264	+ 9,582	(1)
Property, Plant and Equipment	40,607	26,507	+ 14,100	(12)
Less: Accumulated depreciation and amortization	(11,528)	(7,530)	+ (3,998)	(6)
Other Assets	373	668	− 295	(10)
Total Assets	$95,298	$75,909	+ 19,389	
Liabilities and Stockholders' Equity				
Total current liabilities	$27,461	$20,432	+ 7,029	(1)
Deferred Federal Income Taxes	843	635	+ 208	(7)
Long-Term Debt	21,059	16,975	+ 4,084	(8) (13)
Common stock	4,803	4,594	+ 209	(9)
Additional paid-in capital	957	910	+ 47	(9)
Retained earnings	40,175	32,363	+ 7,812	(4) (14)
Total Liabilities and Stockholders' Equity	$95,298	$75,909	$ 19,389	

The cost being allocated through depreciation is the original purchase price of a fixed asset, which was accounted for in the statement of changes as a use of funds in the year the asset was purchased. Deducting depreciation expense from net income in the current year's statement of changes would be a form of double-counting the cost. Therefore depreciation expense is added back to net income as one of the adjustments to obtain working capital from operations. Amortization is similar to depreciation—an expense that enters into the determination of net income but which does not require an outflow of working capital—so it also would be added back.[6]

(6) The depreciation and amortization expense for R.E.C., Inc. in 1983, found on the earnings statement, is $3,998 thousand. (The other expenses recorded by R.E.C., Inc.—selling and administrative, advertising, lease payments, repairs and maintenance—all required an outflow of funds, so they properly remain in the computation of net income.) So far, then, we have as sources of working capital from operations for R.E.C., Inc.:

	1983
Net earnings for the year	$9,394
Plus: Depreciation and amortization	3,998

(7) We must next consider our old friend from Chapter 2, **deferred taxes.** Remember that the deferred tax liability was created as a reconciliation between the amount of tax expense reported on the income statement and the cash actually paid to the I.R.S. If the noncurrent[7] deferred tax liability increases from

---

6. Depletion would be handled in the same manner as depreciation and amortization expense.

7. For a statement of changes in financial position prepared on a working capital basis, a change in a "current" deferred tax account would be included in the change in working capital and therefore would not enter into the adjustment of working capital from operations.

one year to the next, tax expense deducted on the earnings statement (to arrive at net income) has exceeded cash paid for taxes. Thus, an increase in the deferred tax liability account is added to obtain working capital from operations. (A decrease in noncurrent deferred tax liabilities would be subtracted.) Now refer to the condensed R.E.C., Inc. balance sheet in Exhibit 4.4 showing the change in the Deferred Federal Income Taxes account:

	$ Change
Deferred Federal Income Taxes	+ 208

The increase in the deferred federal income tax liability is added back to net income; this represents the portion of R.E.C., Inc.'s tax expense that was not actually paid in cash.

	1983
Net earnings for the year	$ 9,394
Depreciation and amortization	3,998
Increase in deferred income taxes—noncurrent	208
Working Capital provided from operations	$13,600

Thus, R.E.C., Inc. internally generated $13,600 thousand in working capital during 1983.

There are other items (not present for R.E.C., Inc.) that enter into the net income adjustment to obtain working capital provided by operations. One such item is the recognition of investment income in unconsolidated subsidiaries under the equity method of accounting, discussed on pages 64–66. When a company uses the equity method, earnings are recognized (and included in the determination of net income) beyond the receipt of cash dividends. Again, this is a situation where net earnings do not jibe with operating working capital because earnings have been recorded in excess of the inflow of cash. For a firm using the equity method to account for investments in unconsolidated subsidiaries, there would be a deduction from net income (to the extent that earnings recognized surpass dividends received) to obtain working capital from operations. Other adjustment items include account changes relating to deferred income, deferred expense, the amortization of bond discounts and premiums, and extraordinary items.

After working capital from operations, we consider the funds provided from external sources, that is, separate from the selling of goods and services that comprise the operations of a business. Typical external sources of funds are long-term borrowing, issuance of common or preferred stock, sale of or retirement of fixed assets, and the sale of property.

(8) **Additions to long-term debt.** Reference to the R.E.C., Inc. statement of changes reveals that the first "other" source of funds is long-term borrowing. The actual amount of the change in long-term debt is determined by an examination of the long-term debt account from Exhibit 4.4:

	$ Change
Long-Term Debt	+ 4,084

Now consider the source of funds, "additions to long-term debt," on the R.E.C., Inc. statement of changes in financial position. The change in long-term debt ($4,084) does not match the statement of changes figure for additions to long-term debt ($5,600). Explaining the cause of the mismatch requires searching through **(11) Uses of working capital,** one of which is **(13) Reductions of long-term debt** ($1,516). What we now have found is

	1983
Additions to long-term debt	$ 5,600
Less: Reductions of long-term debt	(1,516)
Change in long-term debt (Exhibit 4.4)	$ 4,084

and this figure does balance to the change in long-term debt on the balance sheet. Determining the derivation of these two numbers for "additions" and "reductions" involves calculations from Note C—Long-Term Debt to the R.E.C., Inc. financial statements—where detail on the various long-term notes is provided.[8]

(9) Sales of common stock. Through the exercise of stock options, R.E.C., Inc. issued new shares of stock during 1983. The total funds generated from stock sales amounted to $256 thousand. Note that the two accounts on the balance sheet, Common stock and Additional paid-in capital, combine to explain this change (Exhibit 4.4):

	$ Change
Common stock	+ 209
Additional paid-in captial	+ 47
	+ 256

(10) Other sources. This category is a catch-all for any other transactions that provided sources of working capital. In the case of R.E.C., Inc. the other sources stem from a decrease in the "Other Assets" account on the balance sheet, which represent holdings in investment properties. The sale of properties generated $295 thousand in 1983 (Exhibit 4.4):

	$ Change
Other Assets	− 295

(Remember that the decrease in an asset account is a source of funds.)

(11) Uses of working capital are the various events and transactions that result in the application of funds. The major uses of working capital are 1) a loss from operations, 2) the purchase of noncurrent assets, 3) the reduction of

---

8. (From Note C—Long-Term Debt)

1983	1982	Additions	Reductions
$3,808,000	$4,174,000	$ —	$ 366,000
4,800,000	5,200,000	$ —	400,000
6,000,000	6,750,000	$ —	750,000
2,367,000	2,367,000	—	—
5,968,000		$5,968,000	
Less change in current maturities		(368,000)	
		$5,600,000	$1,516,000

long-term debt, 4) the retirement of capital stock, and 5) the payment of dividends on capital stock. R.E.C., Inc. has recorded three categories of funds applications: additions to property, plant, and equipment; the reduction of long-term debt; and the payment of cash dividends on common stock.

(12) Additions to property, plant, and equipment represent a net addition to R.E.C., Inc.'s buildings, leasehold improvements, and equipment in the amount of $14,100 thousand (Exhibit 4.4):

	$ Change
Property, Plant and Equipment	+ 14,100

Two points of clarification are needed. First, the account change is based on the figure for gross property, plant, and equipment rather than the amount net of accumulated depreciation and amortization (which are part of the adjustment to determine working capital provided by operations). Secondly, complications can arise when a company both adds to and retires or sells items in this category in the same year. For instance, a firm might purchase a new machine, which necessitates selling an old machine. There would be both a use of funds (the purchase) and a source of funds (the sale) shown separately in the statement; the two transactions would (or should) net to the change in the gross property, plant, and equipment account.

(13) Reductions of long-term debt were mentioned earlier in connection with "additions to long-term debt" as a source of funds. During 1983, R.E.C., Inc. reduced some of its long-term debt and added a new long-term note. The footnote on page 81 shows the computation of the additions and reductions from Note C of the R.E.C., Inc. financial statements. The additions (source) and reductions (use) net to the change in the long-term debt account:

	1983
Additions to long-term debt	$ 5,600
Less: Reductions of long-term debt	(1,516)
Change in long-term debt (Exhibit 4.4)	$ 4,084

(14) Cash dividends. The final use of funds listed on R.E.C., Inc.'s statement of changes in financial position is the payment of cash dividends on common stock in the amount of $1,582 thousand during 1983. The 1983 net income figure less the cash dividends paid explain the change in the retained earnings account:

	1983
Net earnings	$9,394
Less: Cash dividends	1,582
Change in retained earnings (Exhibit 4.4)	$7,812

Summary. For R.E.C., Inc., in 1983 working capital increased by $2,553 thousand, the amount by which total sources of working capital ($19,751 thousand) exceeded total uses of working capital ($17,198 thousand). The sources and uses of working capital were obtained through an analysis of the change in each balance sheet account for R.E.C., Inc. between year-end 1982 and 1983.

Assets	$ Change	Explanation	
Total current assets	+ 9,582	Change in working capital	
Property, Plant and Equipment	+14,100	Use of working capital	
Accumulated depreciation and amortization	+(3,998)	Added to net income to obtain working capital from operations (source)	
Other Assets	− 295	Source of working capital	
Liabilities and Stockholders' Equity			
Total current liabilities	+ 7,029	Change in working capital	
Deferred Federal Income Taxes	+ 208	Added to net income to obtain working capital from operations (source)	
Long-Term Debt	+ 4,084	Additions (source)	5,600
		Reductions (use)	(1,516)
		Net change	4,084
Common Stock	+ 209	Source of working capital	
Additional paid-in capital	+ 47	Source of working capital	
Retained earnings	+ 7,812	Net income (source)	9,394
		Cash dividends (use)	1,582
		Net change	7,812

(15) Changes in components of working capital. The bottom portion of the statement of changes in financial position for R.E.C., Inc. lists the change in each current asset and current liability account (see Exhibit 4.5). The increase in working capital (shown at the end of the statements) is $2,553 thousand in 1983 (it is the same balancing figure shown in the middle of the statement). The increase in working capital results from the net addition to current assets of $9,582 thousand less the net addition to current liabilities of $7,029 thousand. The component changes shown for the 1983 column are calculated from the ending balance sheet current asset and current liability accounts for 1983 relative to 1982.

R.E.C., Inc.   **Exhibit 4.5**
Consolidated Statements of Changes in Financial Position
For the years ended December 31, 1983, 1982, and 1981
(In thousands)

	1983	1982	1981
(15) Changes in components of working capital			
Increase (decrease) in current assets			
Cash	$ 1,679	(235)	$ 782
Marketable securities	(2,732)	(1,841)	976
Accounts receivable—net	610	3,339	448
Inventories	10,272	7,006	2,331
Prepaid expenses	(247)	(295)	82
	9,582	7,974	4,619
Increase (decrease) in current liabilities			
Accounts payable	6,703	(1,051)	902
Notes payable—banks	(398)	1,931	1,452
Current maturities of long-term debt	368	(77)	(126)
Accrued liabilities	356	(1,696)	(927)
	7,029	(893)	1,301
Increase in Working Capital	$ 2,553	$ 8,867	$3,318

Exhibit 4.6 R.E.C., Inc.
Partial Balance Sheet at December 31, 1983 and 1982
(In thousands)

	1983	1982	$ Change
Current Assets			
Cash	$ 4,061	$ 2,382	+ 1,679
Marketable securities	5,272	8,004	− 2,732
Accounts receivable—net	8,960	8,350	+ 610
Inventories	47,041	36,769	+ 10,272
Prepaid expenses	512	759	− 247
Total current assets	$65,846	$56,264	+ 9,582
Current Liabilities			
Accounts payable	$14,294	$ 7,591	+ 6,703
Notes payable—banks	5,614	6,012	− 398
Current maturities of long-term debt	1,884	1,516	+ 368
Accrued liabilities	5,669	5,313	+ 356
Total current liabilities	$27,461	$20,432	+ 7,029

Exhibit 4.6 is a partial balance sheet for R.E.C., Inc., presenting only the current asset and current liability accounts. The last column of Exhibit 4.6 shows the change (in thousands of dollars) between year-end 1982 and 1983 of each account and is the same information provided on the statement of changes in financial position for 1983. The component section enables the analyst to determine how each of the working capital accounts impacted on the overall change in working capital. These figures will be used to compute cash flow from operations later in this chapter.

Analyzing the Data

What does it all mean? The Cheshire Cat, you will recall, told Alice she would get somewhere if only she walked long enough. The "somewhere" in this case is "useful information for financial decisions." The analysis of financial statements will be covered in Chapter 5, but it should be of interest—after all the hard work of understanding how the statement of changes is prepared—to preview what it can tell us of practical significance.

The first important fact is that R.E.C., Inc. has increased working capital in 1981, 1982, and 1983. Working capital is one measure of liquidity (the ability of the firm to meet demands for cash), because working capital is the amount by which current assets exceed current liabilities. Current assets are potential cash resources, while current liabilities are prospective cash drains. The statement also reveals the proportion of a firm's funds that are generated from operations as opposed to other financing sources:

R.E.C., Inc.
Percent of Total Sources of Working Capital

	1983	1982	1981
Working Capital provided by operations	68.9%	52.8%	91.9%
Additions to long-term debt	28.3	46.1	6.8
Sales of common stock	1.3	1.1	1.3
Other sources	1.5	—	—
Total	100.0%	100.0%	100.0%

R.E.C., Inc. has had to rely more heavily on long-term debt financing in its two most recent years, particularly in 1982 when external borrowing contributed almost half (46.1%) of the firm's total sources of working capital. The internal generation of funds improved somewhat in 1983, with working capital from operations providing almost 70% of total funds.

On the uses side, R.E.C., Inc. has substantially increased the proportion of funds applied to investments in fixed assets:

R.E.C., Inc.
Percent of Total Uses of Working Capital

	1983	1982	1981
Additions to property, plant, and equipment	82.0%	58.0%	66.9%
Reductions of long-term debt	8.8	19.4	2.1
Cash dividends	9.2	22.6	31.0
Total	100.0%	100.0%	100.0%

In 1983, additions to property, plant, and equipment accounted for over 80% of total funds used. There has been a corresponding decline in the percentage of funds applied to the payment of cash dividends. The implications and explanations of these policies will be explored in Chapter 5.

CASH FLOW FROM OPERATIONS

It is possible for a firm to be profitable and go bankrupt. It is possible for a firm to generate working capital from operations and go bankrupt. How? Alice apparently has still farther to walk on her journey! The problem is cash. Net income does not measure cash flow, nor does working capital from operations (in spite of the fact that some analysts use "net income plus depreciation" as a proxy for cash flow). Why is cash flow from operations important, and where can the amount of cash flow be found in the financial statements? These are the questions we will attempt to answer in the remainder of the chapter.

Importance

1. You are a banker, and you are considering a loan request from a prospective customer. What is your primary concern in making a decision regarding approval or denial of the loan request?

2. You are a wholesaler of goods and have been asked to sell your products on credit to a potential buyer. What is the major determining factor regarding approval or denial of the credit sale?

3. You are an employee and expect to be paid at the end of the month. What must be present in order for your company to meet its payroll?

The answers to all three questions relate to cash:

1. The banker must judge whether or not the prospective borrower will be able to service its debt by making interest and principal payments when they are due.

2. The wholesaler will sell goods on credit only to those customers expected to pay their accounts.

3. A company can meet its employee payroll only if the necessary cash is available.

The ongoing operations of any business firm depend on its ability to generate cash from business operations. It is cash that a firm needs to pay its bills and service its debt. Temporary shortfalls of cash can be satisfied by borrowing, but ultimately a company must generate cash to repay the borrowed funds.

Cash flow from operations has become increasingly important in recent years as an analytical tool to determine the financial health of a business enterprise.[9] Long periods of high interest rates and inflation have contributed to the enhanced attention paid to cash flow by investors and creditors. High interest rates can put the cost of borrowing to cover short-term cash needs out of the reach of many firms seeking to cover temporary cash shortages. Inflation has so distorted the meaningfulness of net income, through the understatement of depreciation and cost of goods sold expenses, that other measures of operating performance and financial success have become essential. Why is the conventional net income figure inadequate to satisfy financial analysts?

The Nocash Corp.

The Nocash Corp. had sales of $100,000 in its second year of operations, up from $50,000 in the first year. Expenses (including taxes) amounted to $70,000 in Year 2, compared with $40,000 in Year 1. The comparative income statements for the two years indicate a substantial improvement, with Year 2 earnings three times greater than those reported in Year 1.

Nocash Corporation
Income Statement for Year 1 and Year 2

	Year 1	Year 2
Sales	$50,000	$100,000
Expenses	40,000	70,000
Net income	$10,000	$ 30,000

There are some additional facts, which are relevant to Nocash's operations but which do not appear in the income statement:

---

9. For additional reading on this topic, see L. M. Fraser, "Cash Flow From Operations and Liquidity Analysis: A New Financial Ratio for Commercial Lending Decisions," *The Journal of Commercial Bank Lending,* November 1983; J. E. Perry, "Cash Flow—the Most Critical Issue of the 1980s," *The Journal of Commercial Banking Lending,* September 1982; J. W. Ketz and R. F. Kochanek, "Cash Flow: Assessing a Company's Real Financial Health," *Financial Executive,* July 1982; R. Greene, "Are More Chryslers in the Offing?" *Forbes,* February 2, 1981; J. A. Largay and C. P. Stickney, "Cash Flows, Ratio Analysis, and the W. T. Grant Bankruptcy," *Financial Analysts Journal,* July-August, 1980.

1. In order to improve sales in Year 2, Nocash eased its credit policies and attracted customers of a substantially lower quality than in Year 1.

2. Nocash purchased a new line of inventory near the end of Year 1; it became apparent during Year 2 that the inventory would be unsalable, except at substantial reductions below cost.

3. Rumors regarding Nocash's problems with regard to accounts receivable and inventory management prompted many suppliers to refuse the sale of goods on credit to Nocash.

The effect of these factors can be found on the Nocash balance sheet.

Nocash Corp.
Balance Sheet at 12/31

	Year 1	Year 2	$ Change	
Cash	$10,000	$10,000	—	
Accounts Receivable	10,000	30,000	+20,000	(1)
Inventories	10,000	25,000	+15,000	(2)
Total Assets	$30,000	$65,000	+35,000	
Accounts Payable	$15,000	$10,000	− 5,000	(3)
Notes Payable to Banks	—	10,000	+10,000	
Equity	15,000	45,000	+30,000	
Total Liabilities and Equity	$30,000	$65,000	+35,000	

(1) Accounts receivable increased (at a faster pace than sales) as the result of a deterioration in customer quality. (2) Ending inventory also rose and included items that would ultimately be sold at a loss. (3) Nocash's inability to purchase goods on credit from suppliers caused a net reduction in the balance of accounts payable.

If we were to recalculate net income on a cash basis, the following adjustments would be made, using the dollar change (between Year 1 and Year 2) in ending accounts balances:

Net income	$30,000
(1) Accounts receivable	(20,000)
(2) Inventories	(15,000)
(3) Accounts payable	(5,000)
Cash flow	($10,000)

(1) The increase in accounts receivable is subtracted because more sales revenue was recognized in computing net income than was collected in cash.

Sales recognized in net income		$100,000
Sales collected:		
Beginning accounts receivable	$ 10,000	
Plus: Sales, Year 2	100,000	
Less: Ending accounts receivable	(30,000)	80,000
Difference between net income and cash flow		$ 20,000

(2) The increase in inventories is deducted, reflecting the cash outflow for inventory purchases in excess of the expense recognized through cost of goods sold.

Purchases for inventory*	$75,000
Less: Cost of goods sold	60,000
Difference between net income and cash flow	$15,000

(3) The decrease in accounts payable is deducted because the cash payments to suppliers in Year 2 were greater than the amount of expense recorded. (In essence, cash was paid for some Year 1 accounts as well as Year 2 accounts.)

Payments to suppliers**	$80,000
Purchases for inventory*	75,000
Difference between net income and cash flow	$ 5,000

How did Nocash cover its $10,000 cash shortfall? The astute reader will have noticed the appearance of a $10,000 note payable to banks on the Year 2 balance sheet. The bank borrowing has enabled Nocash to continue to operate, but unless the company can begin to generate cash from operations its problems will compound.

Finding Cash Flow from Operations It is a simple process to find cash flow from operations in the financial statements of those companies that prepare the statement of changes in financial position on a cash basis. (See Exhibit 4.8 for the illustration of a cash basis statement.) Cash flow from operations is the first item under sources of funds in the statement of changes in financial position that defines ''funds'' as cash. Most firms, however, use the working capital concept of funds, and cash flow from operations must be calculated from data presented in the statement of changes in financial position. To illustrate this calculation, we will return to the R.E.C., Inc. Consolidated Statements of Changes in Financial Position.

Two steps are involved to determine cash flow from operations, but one has already been taken: (1) net income must be adjusted for items (such as depreciation expense), which did not involve an inflow or outflow of working capital to arrive at working capital from operations; and (2) the figure for working capital from operations is then adjusted for changes in the current accounts (such as accounts receivable and inventories) that affect cash flow.

---

*Ending inventory	$25,000
Plus: Cost of goods sold	60,000
Less: Beginning inventory	(10,000)
Purchases	$75,000
Beginning accounts payable	$15,000
Plus: Purchases	75,000
Less: Ending accounts payable	(10,000)
**Payments	$80,000

(1) The statement of changes in financial position contains the first adjustment (net income to working capital provided from operations), so we will begin with working capital provided from operations for R.E.C., Inc.:

	1983	1982	1981
Working Capital provided from operations	$13,600	$9,030	$8,515

and (2) adjust this amount for changes in those current assets and current liabilities that relate to the firm's operations and affect cash. To make the adjustment, we will use two general rules.

Include in the adjustment all current accounts except cash, cash equivalents (marketable securities), and nonoperating accounts such as notes receivable (other than from customers), notes payable (other than to suppliers), and current maturities of long-term debt.   Rule I

For R.E.C., Inc., these include accounts receivable, inventories, prepaid expenses, accounts payable, and accrued liabilities. Current accounts not included in the adjustment are cash and cash equivalents (marketable securities) because these are the accounts explained by a cash basis statement; notes payable to banks and current maturities of long-term debt are not included because these are financing sources outside the normal operations of the business.

Add: − current assets, + current liabilities   Rule II
Subtract: + current assets, − current liabilities

Add back to working capital from operations the decrease in a current asset account or the increase in a current liability account. Subtract the increase in a current asset or the decrease in a current liability account. For example, consider the following account changes for 1983 from the "changes in components of working capital" (balance sheet account changes between 12–31–82 and 12–31–83) of the R.E.C., Inc. Consolidated Statements of Changes in Financial Position:

	1983
Changes in components of working capital	
Increase (decrease) in current assets	
Cash	$ 1,679
Marketable securities	(2,732)
*Accounts receivable–net	610
*Inventories	10,272
*Prepaid expenses	(247)
	$ 9,582
Increase (decrease) in current liabilities	
*Accounts payable	$ 6,703
Notes payable–banks	(398)
Current maturities of long-term debt	368
*Accrued liabilities	356
	7,029
Increase in working capital	$ 2,553

The accounts marked with an asterisk are included in the adjustment. The increase in accounts receivable of $610 thousand would be subtracted because, as was the case for Nocash Corp., the net increase represents sales made and recognized in net income but not yet collected in cash. The increase in inventories is subtracted, the decrease in prepaid expenses is added, the increase in accounts payable is added, and the increase in accrued liabilities is added.

Exhibit 4.7 presents the adjustment of R.E.C., Inc.'s working capital provided from operations to cash flow provided from operations for the years ended December 31, 1983, 1982, and 1981. (Also included for clarification is Exhibit 4.8, which is a complete cash basis statement for the year ended December 31, 1983.)

The first point of significance is the negative cash flow from operations generated by R.E.C., Inc. for 1982 ($3,767 thousand). It should be noted that

Exhibit 4.7   **R.E.C., Inc.**
Cash Flow from Operations for Years Ended December 31, 1983, 1982, and 1981

	1983	1982	1981
Working Capital provided from operations	$13,600	$9,030	$8,515
Accounts receivable—net	− 610	−3,339	− 448
Inventories	−10,272	−7,006	−2,331
Prepaid expenses	+ 247	+ 295	− 82
Accounts payable	+ 6,703	−1,051	+ 902
Accrued liabilities	+ 356	−1,696	− 927
Cash Flow provided from operations	$10,024	($3,767)	$5,629

Exhibit 4.8   **R.E.C., Inc.**
Consolidated Statement of Changes in Financial Position
For the year ended December 31, 1983
(In thousands)

Sources of cash	
From operations	$10,024
Additions to long-term debt*	5,968
Sales of common stock	256
Other sources	295
Total Sources	$16,543
Uses of cash	
Additions to property, plant, and equipment	$14,100
Reductions of short-term debt	398
Reductions of long-term debt	1,516
Cash dividends	1,582
Total Uses	$17,596
Decrease in cash and cash equivalents	$ 1,053**

*Includes increase in current maturities.

**Cash increase 12/31/82 to 12/31/83	$1,679
Marketable securities decrease 12/31/82 to 12/31/83	(2,732)
	$(1,053)

the *negative cash flow* occurred for a year in which the firm reported *positive net earnings* of $5,910 thousand and *positive working capital from operations* of $9,030 thousand. The cash flow crunch was apparently caused primarily by a substantial growth in accounts receivable and inventories. The second major revelation is that R.E.C., Inc. was able to recover in 1983, returning to a strongly positive generator of cash, in spite of a continuation of the buildup in inventories. (In 1983, R.E.C., Inc.'s sales grew at a more rapid pace than inventories.) It will be necessary to monitor R.E.C., Inc's cash flow from operations closely in the future, and, in particular, the firm's management of inventories. Inventory growth is desirable when supporting an expansion of sales but is undesirable when, like the Nocash Corp. example, the inventory is not selling.

The adjustment of working capital to cash flow from operations illustrated for R.E.C., Inc. can be made for any company from its statement of changes in financial position, using the rules and procedures outlined in the example. Cash flow from operations is especially important for those firms that are heavily invested in inventories and that use trade account receivables and payables as a major part of ordinary business operations and therefore should be a critical ingredient in the credit or investment analysis of such firms. The existence of obsolete or slow-moving inventory, a rise of accounts receivable of inferior quality, and the tightening of credit by suppliers can all lead to severe cash flow problems and, ultimately, bankruptcy.

A WALK LONG ENOUGH!

Alice, the Cheshire Cat, and the reader must surely be exhausted by now. It is hoped that the chapter has provided adequate enlightenment regarding the statement of changes in financial position and cash flow from operations. An appropriate conclusion to the chapter is the continuation of the conversation between the Cheshire Cat and Alice before she resumed her journey.

CHESHIRE CAT: . . . we're all mad here. I'm mad. You're mad.

ALICE: How do you know I'm mad?

CHESHIRE CAT: You must be, or you wouldn't have come here![10]

---

10. Lewis Carroll, *op cit.*, p. 90.

SELF-TEST   Solutions are provided in Appendix D.

_____ 1. Where, in the annual report, can one gain information about the generation of cash from operations?
   (a) The notes to the financial statements.
   (b) The balance sheet.
   (c) The statement of changes in financial position.
   (d) The earnings statement.

_____ 2. What does the statement of changes in financial position summarize for a firm?
   (a) The financing and investing activities for a period.
   (b) The change in financial position from one period to the next.
   (c) The change in earnings per share.
   (d) Both (a) and (b).

_____ 3. What are funds?
   (a) Current assets plus current liabilities.
   (b) Working capital or cash.
   (c) Cash or current liabilities.
   (d) Short-term investments.

_____ 4. Why is the statement of changes in financial position extremely useful to the financial analyst?
   (a) It provides insight into managements' financial policies and strategies.
   (b) It discloses net income for a period.
   (c) It explains the increase in current assets.
   (d) It is prepared on a cash basis.

_____ 5. What does a statement of changes in financial position prepared on a "cash" basis explain?
   (a) The difference between current assets and current liabilities.
   (b) The change in working capital.
   (c) The change in the balance sheet cash account or cash plus cash equivalents account for an accounting period.
   (d) None of the above.

_____ 6. What is the balancing equation for the statement of changes in financial position?
   (a) Sources + Uses = Change in Cash or Working Capital.
   (b) Sources − Uses = Change in Cash or Working Capital.
   (c) Current Assets + Current Liabilities = Change in Cash or Working Capital.
   (d) Sources = Assets − Liabilities and Equity.

7. What is working capital? _____
   (a) The amount by which current assets exceed current liabilities.
   (b) The amount by which assets exceed liabilities.
   (c) The amount by which cash exceeds liabilities.
   (d) The amount by which cash exceeds cash equivalents.

8. On what basis is the statement of changes in financial position usually _____ prepared?
   (a) Accrual basis.
   (b) Cash basis.
   (c) Working capital basis.
   (d) Current basis.

9. Which of the following is a financing activity that does not affect cash or _____ working capital?
   (a) Increase of accounts receivable.
   (b) Long-term borrowing.
   (c) Issuance of common stock.
   (d) Conversion of bonds into common stock.

10. Which of the following is not a primary source of working capital? _____
    (a) Revenue from operations.
    (b) Long-term borrowing.
    (c) Issuance of equity securities.
    (d) Disposal of current liabilities.

11. What are "internally" generated funds? _____
    (a) Funds converted to cash.
    (b) Funds provided by the firm's normal business activities.
    (c) Funds provided by extraordinary events.
    (d) Funds retained by the firm.

12. How is working capital from operations determined? _____
    (a) Net earnings less dividends paid.
    (b) Net earnings adjusted for items that did not use or provide working capital.
    (c) Net earnings adjusted for uses of working capital.
    (d) Net earnings less depreciation.

13. Which of the following would not be used to adjust net income to obtain _____ working capital from operations?
    (a) Depreciation.
    (b) Deferred taxes.
    (c) Lease payments.
    (d) Amortization of bond discounts and premiums.

_____ 14. Which of the following would be considered an external source of funds?
   (a) Issuance of common stock.
   (b) Sale of fixed assets.
   (c) Long-term borrowing.
   (d) All of the above.

_____ 15. Which of the following is not a major use of working capital?
   (a) The addition of long-term debt.
   (b) The payment of dividends on capital stock.
   (d) A loss from operations
   (d) The purchase of noncurrent assets.

_____ 16. The statement of changes in financial position reveals several items of significance. Which of the following is not revealed in the statement?
   (a) Profitability of the firm is revealed by the change in net working capital.
   (b) Liquidity of the firm is revealed by the working capital amount.
   (c) The proportion of a firm's funds that are generated from operations.
   (d) The proportion of funds used for investments in fixed assets.

_____ 17. How is it possible for a firm to be profitable and still go bankrupt?
   (a) Earnings have increased more rapidly than sales.
   (b) The firm has positive net income figures, but has not generated sufficient cash to support operations.
   (c) Net income adjusted for inflation can cause a firm to go bankrupt.
   (d) Sales are not improved even though credit policies are eased.

_____ 18. Why has cash flow from operations become increasingly important in recent years as an analytical tool to determine the financial status of a firm?
   (a) Inflation has distorted the meaningfulness of the net income figure.
   (b) High interest rates can put the cost of borrowing to cover short-term cash needs out of reach for many firms.
   (c) Firms could have uncollectible accounts receivable and unsalable inventory on its books, which will not generate cash.
   (d) All of the above.

_____ 19. Under Rule I, for determining cash flow from operations, which account would be included in the adjustment?
   (a) Accounts receivable.
   (b) Cash.
   (c) Cash Equivalents.
   (d) Current maturities of long-term debt.

20. What is Rule II for adjusting working capital from operations to determine _____ cash flow from operations?
    (a) Add decreases in current accounts; subtract increases in noncurrent accounts.
    (b) Add decreases in current asset accounts and increases in current liability accounts; subtract increases in current asset accounts and decreases in current liability accounts.
    (c) Add increases in current asset and liability accounts; subtract decreases in current asset and liability accounts.
    (d) Add changes in all current asset accounts; subtract changes in all current liability accounts.

21. Which of the following statements is false in regard to cash flow from _____ operations?
    (a) A negative cash flow can occur in a year when net earnings as well as working capital are positive.
    (b) Increases in current asset accounts represent items not yet collected in cash.
    (c) Increases in current liability accounts represent items not yet collected in cash.
    (d) Working capital from operations should be adjusted by all current accounts except cash, cash equivalents, and nonoperating accounts to determine cash flow from operations.

22. Which of the following items could lead to cash flow problems? _____
    (a) Obsolete inventory, accounts receivable of inferior quality, easing of credit by suppliers.
    (b) Slow-moving inventory, accounts receivable of inferior quality, tightening of credit by suppliers.
    (c) Obsolete inventory, increasing notes payable, easing of credit by suppliers.
    (d) Obsolete inventory, a decrease of accounts receivable of inferior quality, slow-moving inventory.

23. Below are items found on a statement of changes in financial position. Mark sources of working capital with an ''S,'' uses of working capital with a ''U,'' and items not using or providing working capital with an ''N.''
    (a) Purchase of equipment _____
    (b) Disposal of noncurrent assets _____
    (c) Exchange of property _____
    (d) Net income _____
    (e) Cash dividend payments _____
    (f) Reduction of long-term debt _____
    (g) Additions to long-term borrowing _____
    (h) Conversion of bonds into stock _____
    (i) Issuance of equity securities _____
    (j) Purchase of land _____

24. Mark items that are operating accounts with an "0" and mark items that are nonoperating accounts with an "N" under Rule I for adjusting working capital from operations to cash flow from operations.

_____ (a) Accounts Receivable
_____ (b) Marketable securities
_____ (c) Accrued liabilities
_____ (d) Cash
_____ (e) Inventories
_____ (f) Current maturities of long-term debt
_____ (g) Prepaid expenses
_____ (h) Notes payable—banks
_____ (i) Accounts payable
_____ (j) Notes receivable—officers

25. When adjusting working capital from operations to determine cash flow from operations, will the following items be added or subtracted? Mark additions with "A" and subtractions with "S."

_____ (a) Decrease in accounts receivable
_____ (b) Increase in inventories
_____ (c) Increase in prepaid expenses
_____ (d) Increase in accounts payable
_____ (e) Decrease in accrued liabilities

26. The following information is available for Jacqui's Jewelry and Gift Store:

Working Capital from operations	$10,000
Decrease in accounts receivable	2,000
Increase in inventories	9,000
Decrease in accounts payable	5,000
Increase in accrued liabilities	1,000

_____ What is cash flow from operations?
(a) $(1,000)
(b) $4,000
(c) $13,000
(d) $5,000

27. Recalculate net income on a cash basis based on the following information for St. Clair Sports Apparel, Inc.:

Net income (accrual basis)	$50,000
Increase in accounts receivable	10,000
Increase in inventories	5,000
Decrease in accounts payable	5,000

(a) $70,000
(b) $50,000
(c) $30,000
(d) $60,000

28. From the following information for MTF Company, calculate the change _____ in working capital:

Change in components of working capital:	
Increase (decrease) in current assets	
Cash	$2,000
Accounts Receivable	(700)
Inventories	5,000
	$6,300
Increase (decrease) in current liabilities	
Accounts Payable	$7,000
Notes payable-banks	(1,000)
Current maturities of long-term debt	(2,000)
	$4,000

(a) Increase in working capital = $2,300.
(b) Decrease in working capital = $2,300.
(c) Increase in working capital = $2,700.
(d) Decrease in working capital = $2,700.

The Analysis of 5
Financial Statements

This book began with the supposition that financial statements contain information about the financial condition, operating success, and future potential of a business enterprise. In the preceding chapters we have examined in detail the form and content of the four basic financial statements found in the annual reports of American firms: the balance sheet, the income statement, the statement of retained earnings or statement of shareholders' equity, and the statement of changes in financial position. The next step is to determine how we can use such information to make sound (and hopefully profitable) business decisions. The purpose of financial statement analysis is exactly that: to convert financial statement data into useful information.

Before beginning the analysis of any set of financial statements, it is necessary to specify the objectives of the analysis. Objectives vary depending on the perspective of the financial statement user and the particular questions that are addressed by the analysis of the financial statement data.

Objective

A *creditor* is ultimately concerned with the ability of an existing or prospective borrower to repay interest and principal on borrowed funds. The types of questions raised in credit analyses are:

- What is the borrowing cause? What do the financial statement numbers reveal about the reason a firm has requested a loan or the purchase of supplies on credit?

- What is the firm's capital structure? How much debt is currently outstanding? How well has debt been serviced in the past?

- How liquid is the firm? What will be the source of debt repayment? How well does the company manage working capital? Is the firm generating cash flow from operations?

The credit analyst must use the historical record of the company, as presented through the financial statements, to answer such questions and to predict the potential of the firm to satisfy future demands for cash, including debt service.

The *investor* attempts to arrive at an estimation of a company's future earnings stream in order to attach a value to the securities being considered for purchase or liquidation. The investment analyst poses questions such as:

- How well has the company performed in the past, and what are its future expectations? What is its record with regard to growth and stability of earnings?

- How much risk is inherent in the firm's existing capital structure? What returns can an investor expect, given its current condition and future outlook?

- How successfully does the firm compete in its industry, and how well positioned is the company to hold or improve its competitive position?

The investment analyst also uses historical financial statement data to forecast the future. In the case of the investor, the objective is to determine whether an investment is warranted.

Financial statement analysis from the standpoint of *management* relates to all of the above questions raised by creditors and investors because these user groups must be satisfied in order for the firm to obtain capital as needed. Management must also consider its employees, the general public, regulators, the financial press, and others. Management looks to the financial data to find out:

- How well has the firm performed and why? What operating areas have contributed to success and which have not?

- What are the strengths and weaknesses of the company's financial position?

- What changes should be implemented in order to improve future performance?

Financial statements provide insight into the company's current status and lead to the development of policies and strategies for the future. It should be pointed out, however, that management also has responsibility for preparing the financial statements published in a corporate annual report. The analyst should be alert to the potential for management to influence the outcome of the financial statement numbers in order to appeal to creditors, investors, and other users of the data. (See the discussion of this topic in Chapter 1 and Appendix A.) It is important that any analysis of financial statements include a careful reading of the notes to the financial statements, and it may be helpful to supplement the analysis with other material in the annual report and with sources of information apart from the annual report itself.

Sources of Data   The financial statement user has access to a wide range of data sources in the performance of an analysis of financial statements. The objective of the analysis will dictate to a considerable extent not only the approach taken in the analysis but also the particular sources that should be used in a given circumstance. Obviously, the financial statements themselves and the notes to the financial statements are the most important ingredients. Other items in a corporate annual report should be read as well.

Turn first to the report of the independent auditor. This report contains the expression of an opinion as to the fairness of the financial statement presentation. Most auditors' reports are "unqualified," which means that in the opinion of the auditor the financial statements present fairly the financial position, the results of operations, and the changes in financial position. A "qualified" report is a signal that the auditors are, for some reason, not completely satisfied with the financial statements. Qualified reports result from failure to use generally accepted accounting principles, inconsistency in the application of accounting principles, or uncertainties regarding the outcome of significant factors that will affect the ongoing operations of the firm.

Whereas the auditors are "independent," it should be noted that they are employed by the firm being audited. If management doesn't like what the auditors report, the firm can switch auditors. Penn Square was a $500 million (total assets) bank, which failed in July, 1982. Prior to its collapse, the bank fired its auditing firm. The auditor had qualified the report on the bank's financial statements for 1980 due to questionable loan practices. The bank hired a new auditor in March, 1982, and the new auditors issued an unqualified opinion on the 1981 financial statements and removed the qualification from the 1980 statements. Sixteen weeks later the bank failed.[1] A change in auditors should be a signal that there may be serious problems with a company, and the analyst will want to determine why a switch in auditors has been made.

Auditor's Report

"Management's Discussion and Analysis of the Financial Condition and Results of Operations" is a section of the annual report that is required and monitored by the Securities and Exchange Commission. In this section, management presents a detailed coverage of the firm's liquidity, capital resources, and operations. The material can be especially helpful to the financial analyst because it includes facts and estimates not found elsewhere in the annual report. For example, management is supposed to cover some forward-looking information such as projections of capital expenditures and how the investments will be financed. There is detail about the mix of price relative to volume increases for products sold. Management must disclose any favorable or unfavorable trends and any significant events or uncertainties that relate to the firm's historical or prospective financial condition and operations.

Management's Discussion and Analysis

Certain supplementary schedules are required for inclusion in an annual report and are frequently helpful to the financial statement analyst. Large firms must calculate and disclose the impact of inflation on reported earnings. (For a discussion of this topic, see Appendix B.) Companies that operate in several unrelated lines of business show a breakdown of key financial figures by operating segment. (The analysis of segmental data is covered in Appendix C.)

Supplementary Schedules

---

1. "Penn Square Fired Audit Firm After Qualified 1980 Statement," *The American Banker,* July 27, 1982.

Form 10-K   Form 10-K, an annual document filed with the Securities and Exchange Commission by companies that sell securities to the public, contains much of the same financial information as the annual report issued to shareholders. It also shows additional detail that may be of interest to the financial analyst, such as schedules listing management remuneration and transactions, a description of material litigation and governmental actions, and elaborations of many financial statement disclosures. The 10-K report is available to the general public, on request.

References   There is also a considerable body of material outside of the corporate annual report and Form 10-K that can contribute to a thorough analysis of financial statements. Such material can be found in the business reference section of a public or university library. Listed below are sources of comparative statistical ratios to determine a company's relative position within its industry:

1. Dun and Bradstreet, Inc., *Key Business Ratios,* Business Economics Division. New York, N.Y.

2. Robert Morris Associates, *Annual Statement Studies.* Philadelphia, Pa.

3. Standard & Poor's Corporation, *Analyst's Handbook,* and *Industry Surveys.* New York, N.Y.

4. Leo Troy, *Almanac of Business and Industrial Financial Ratios.* Englewood Cliffs, N.J.: Prentice-Hall, Inc.

Also helpful to the analyst are the following references, which contain useful investment and financial information about particular companies and industries:

1. Moody's Investor Service, Inc., *Moody's Manuals.* New York, N.Y.

2. Standard & Poor's Corporation, *Corporation Records* and *Earnings Forecaster.* New York, N.Y.

3. Value Line, Inc., *The Value Line Investment Survey.* New York, N.Y.

Articles from current periodicals such as *Business Week, Forbes, Fortune,* and *The Wall Street Journal* can add insight into the management and operations of individual firms as well as provide perspective on general economic and industry trends.

Tools and Techniques   Various tools and techniques are used by the financial statement analyst in order to convert financial statement data into formats that facilitate the evaluation of a firm's financial condition and performance, both over time and in comparison with industry competitors. These include common size financial statements, which express each account on the balance sheet as a percentage of total assets and each account on the income statement as a percentage of net sales; financial ratios, which standardize financial data in terms of mathematical relationships expressed in the form of percentages or times; trend analysis, which requires the evaluation of financial data over several accounting periods; structural analysis, which looks at the internal structure of a business enterprise; industry comparisons, which relate one firm with averages compiled for the industry in which it operates; and, most important of all, common sense and judgment. These tools and techniques will be illustrated by walking through a financial statement analysis of R.E.C., Inc. The first part will cover "number crunching": the preparation of common size financial statements and the calculation of a set of key financial ratios. The second part will involve the integration of these numbers with other data—such as the statement of changes in financial position and computation of cash flow from operations from Chapter 4—in order to perform an analysis of R.E.C., Inc. over a five-year period, 1979–1983.

NUMBER CRUNCHING

Common Size Financial Statements

Common size financial statements are a form of financial ratio analysis that allows the comparison of firms with different levels of sales or total assets by introducing a common denominator. A common size balance sheet expresses each item on the balance sheet as a percentage of total assets; and a common size income statement expresses each income statement category as a percentage of net sales. Common size statements are also used for the internal or structural analysis of a firm. The common size balance sheet reveals the composition of assets within major categories (for example, cash and cash equivalents relative to other current assets); the distribution of assets in which funds are invested (fixed relative to current); the capital structure of the firm (debt relative to equity); and the debt structure (long-term relative to short-term). The common size income statement shows the relative magnitude of various expenses relative to sales, the profit percentages (gross profit, operating profit, and net profit margins), and the relative importance of "other" revenues and expenses. Common size analysis is used both to evaluate trends and to make industry comparisons. Common size financial statements for R.E.C., Inc. are shown in Exhibits 5.1 and 5.2.

Referring first to the common size balance sheet (Exhibit 5.1), it can be seen that inventories have become increasingly important over the five-year period in the firm's total asset structure and in 1983 comprised almost half (49.4%) of total assets. Holdings of cash and cash equivalents (marketable securities) have declined from a 20% combined level in 1979 and 1980 to about 10% in 1983. R.E.C., Inc. has elected to make this shift in order to accommodate the inventory requirements of new store openings. The company has opened 43 new stores in the past two years, and the effect of this market strategy is also reflected in the fixed asset structure. Buildings, leasehold improvements, equipment, and accumulated depreciation and amortization have increased as a percentage of total assets. On the liability side, the proportion of debt (required to finance the investments in new assets) has risen, primarily from long-term borrowing.

The common size income statement (Exhibit 5.2) reveals the trends of expenses and profit margins. Cost of goods sold, the price R.E.C., Inc. pays

Exhibit 5.1   R.E.C., Inc.
Common Size Balance Sheets
(Percent)

	1983	1982	1981	1980	1979
Assets					
Current Assets					
Cash	4.3	3.1	3.9	5.1	4.9
Marketable securities	5.5	10.6	14.9	15.3	15.1
Accounts receivable less allowance for					
doubtful accounts	9.4	11.0	7.6	6.6	6.8
Inventories	49.4	48.4	45.0	40.1	39.7
Prepaid expenses	.5	1.0	1.6	2.4	2.6
Total current assets	69.1	74.1	73.0	69.5	69.1
Property, Plant, and Equipment					
Land	.8	1.1	1.2	1.4	1.4
Buildings and leashold improvements	19.2	15.7	14.4	14.1	14.5
Equipment	22.6	18.1	17.3	15.9	16.5
Accumulated depreciation and amortization	(12.1)	(9.9)	(6.9)	(3.1)	(3.0)
Net property, plant, and equipment	30.5	25.0	26.0	28.3	29.4
Other Assets	.4	.9	1.0	2.2	1.5
Total Assets	100.0	100.0	100.0	100.0	100.0
Liabilities and Stockholders' Equity					
Current Liabilities					
Accounts payable	15.0	10.0	13.1	11.4	11.8
Notes payable—banks	5.9	7.9	6.2	4.4	4.3
Current maturities of long-term debt	2.0	2.0	2.4	2.4	2.6
Accrued liabilities	5.9	7.0	10.6	7.7	5.7
Total current liabilities	28.8	26.9	32.3	25.9	24.4
Deferred Federal Income Taxes	.9	.8	.7	.5	.4
Long-Term Debt	22.1	22.4	16.2	14.4	14.9
Total liabilities	51.8	50.1	49.2	40.8	39.7
Stockholders' Equity					
Common stock	5.0	6.1	6.7	7.3	7.5
Additional paid-in capital	1.0	1.2	1.3	1.6	1.8
Retained earnings	42.2	42.6	42.8	50.3	51.0
Total stockholders' equity	48.2	49.9	50.8	59.2	60.3
Total Liabilities and Stockholders' Equity	100.0	100.0	100.0	100.0	100.0

to suppliers for the products sold to customers, has risen slightly, resulting in a small decline over the five-year period in the gross profit percentage. To improve this margin the firm will either have to raise its own retail prices or figure ways to cut costs on goods purchased for resale. In the area of operating expenses, lease payments, depreciation, and amortization have increased relative to sales, again reflecting costs associated with new store openings. Selling and administrative expenses also rose in 1981 and 1982, but the company controlled these costs more effectively in 1983. Operating and net profit percentages will be discussed more extensively in connection with the five-year trends of financial ratios later in the chapter. It can be seen from the common size income statement that both profit percentages deteriorated through 1982 and rebounded in the most recent year as R.E.C., Inc. enjoyed the benefits of an economic recovery and profits from expansion.

R.E.C., Inc.   Exhibit 5.2
Common Size Income Statements
(Percent)

	1983	1982	1981	1980	1979
Net sales	100.0	100.0	100.0	100.0	100.0
Cost of goods sold	60.0	60.1	58.0	58.2	58.2
Gross profit	40.0	39.9	42.0	41.8	41.8
Operating Expenses					
Selling and administrative expenses	15.1	17.2	18.1	15.6	15.4
Advertising	6.6	7.1	6.8	6.4	6.3
Lease payments	6.1	4.6	5.1	4.7	4.6
Depreciation and amortization	1.9	2.0	1.8	1.4	1.2
Repairs and maintenance	1.4	1.3	2.2	1.7	1.7
Operating profit	8.9	7.7	8.0	12.0	12.6
Other income (expense)					
Interest income	.2	.5	.5	.3	.3
Interest expense	(1.2)	(1.5)	(.9)	(.9)	(1.0)
Earnings before income taxes	7.9	6.7	7.6	11.4	11.9
Income taxes	3.6	2.9	3.4	5.4	5.7
Net Earnings	4.3	3.8	4.2	6.0	6.2

Using the R.E.C., Inc. financial statements, we will compute a set of key **Key Financial** financial ratios for the years 1983 and 1982. Later, these ratios will be exam- **Ratios** ined in the context of R.E.C., Inc.'s five-year historical record and in comparison with industry standards. The four categories of ratios covered are (1) liquidity ratios, which measure a firm's ability to meet needs for cash as they arise; (2) activity ratios, which measure the liquidity of specific assets; (3) leverage ratios, which measure the extent of a firm's financing with debt relative to equity and its ability to cover interest and other fixed charges; and (4) profitability ratios, which measure the overall performance of a firm and its efficiency in managing assets, liabilities, and equity.

It is desirable to introduce a word of caution before delving into R.E.C., Inc.'s financial ratios. Although extremely useful as analytical tools, financial ratios also have serious limitations. They can serve as screening devices, to point to areas of potential strength or weakness and to indicate matters that need further investigation. But financial ratios do not provide answers in and of themselves, and they are not predictive. Financial ratios should be used along with heavy inputs of common sense and in conjunction with the other elements of a thorough financial statement analysis.

Figures from the R.E.C., Inc. Consolidated Balance Sheets and Statements of Earnings and Retained Earnings (Exhibit 5.3, pages 106 and 107) are used to illustrate the calculation of 17 key financial ratios for 1983 and 1982, and these financial ratios will subsequently be incorporated into an overall financial analysis of the firm.

Exhibit 5.3   R.E.C., Inc.
Consolidated Balance Sheets at December 31, 1983 and 1982
(In thousands)

	1983	1982
Assets		
Current Assets		
Cash	$ 4,061	$ 2,382
Marketable securities (note A)	5,272	8,004
Accounts receivable, less allowance for doubtful accounts of $448 in 1983		
and $417 in 1982	8,960	8,350
Inventories (note A)	47,041	36,769
Prepaid expenses	512	759
Total current assets	65,846	56,264
Property, Plant and Equipment (notes A, C, and E)		
Land	811	811
Buildings and leasehold improvements	18,273	11,928
Equipment	21,523	13,768
	40,607	26,507
Less accumulated depreciation and amortization		
Net property, plant and equipment	11,528	7,530
	29,079	18,977
Other Assets (note A)	373	668
Total Assets	$95,298	$75,909
Liabilities and Stockholders' Equity		
Current Liabilites		
Accounts payable	$14,294	$7,591
Notes payable—banks (note B)	5,614	6,012
Current maturities of long-term debt (note C)	1,884	1,516
Accrued liabilities	5,669	5,313
Total current liabilities	27,461	20,432
Deferred Federal Income Taxes (notes A and D)	843	635
Long-Term Debt (note C)	21,059	16,975
Total liabilities	49,363	38,042
Stockholders' Equity		
Common stock, par value $1, authorized, 10,000,000 shares; issued,		
4,803,000 shares in 1983 and 4,594,000 shares in 1982 (note F)	4,803	4,594
Additional paid-in capital	957	910
Retained earnings	40,175	32,363
Total stockholders' equity	45,935	37,867
Total Liabilities and Stockholders' Equity	$95,298	$75,909

The accompanying notes are an integral part of these statements.

R.E.C., Inc.
Consolidated Statements of Earnings and Retained Earnings
For the Years ended December 31, 1983, 1982, and 1981
(In thousands except per share amounts)

Exhibit 5.3
(Continued)

	1983	1982	1981
Statements of Consolidated Earnings			
Net sales	$215,600	$153,000	$140,700
Cost of goods sold (note A)	129,364	91,879	81,606
Gross profit	86,236	61,121	59,094
Selling and administrative expenses (note A)	32,664	26,382	25,498
Advertising	14,258	10,792	9,541
Lease payments (note E)	13,058	7,111	7,267
Depreciation and amortization (note A)	3,998	2,984	2,501
Repairs and maintenance	3,015	2,046	3,031
Operating profit	19,243	11,806	11,256
Other income (expense)			
Interest income	422	838	738
Interest expense	(2,585)	(2,277)	(1,274)
Earnings before income taxes	17,080	10,367	10,720
Income taxes (notes A and D)	7,686	4,457	4,824
Net Earnings	$ 9,394	$ 5,910	$ 5,896
Earnings per common share (note G)	$1.96	$1.29	$1.33
Statements of Consolidated Retained Earnings			
Retained earnings at beginning of year	$ 32,363	$ 28,315	$ 24,260
Net earnings	9,394	5,910	5,896
Cash dividends (1983—$.33 per share; 1982 and 1981—			
$.41 per share)	(1,582)	(1,862)	(1,841)
Retained earnings at end of year	$ 40,175	$ 32,363	$ 28,315

The accompanying notes are an integral part of these statements.

Current Ratio

	1983	1982
$\dfrac{\text{Current Assets}}{\text{Current Liabilities}}$	$\dfrac{65,846}{27,461} = 2.40$ times	$\dfrac{56,264}{20,432} = 2.75$ times

The current ratio is the most commonly used measure of short-run solvency, the ability of a firm to pay its debts as they come due. Current liabilities (accounts payable, notes payable, current maturities of long-term debt, and accrued liabilities) are used as the denominator of the ratio because they are considered to be the most urgent debts, requiring retirement within a year or an operating cycle. The available cash resources to satisfy these obligations must come primarily from existing cash or the conversion to cash of other current assets (marketable securities, accounts receivable, inventories). Some analysts eliminate prepaid expenses from the numerator because they are not actually a potential source of cash but, rather, represent future obligations that have already been satisfied with cash. The current ratio for R.E.C., Inc. indicates that on December 31, 1983, current assets covered current liabilities 2.4 times, down from year-end 1982. It will be necessary, in order to interpret the significance of this ratio, to evaluate the trend of liquidity over a five-year period and to assess coverage relative to other firms of similar size operating in the same industry. It is also necessary to consider the composition of the components that comprise the ratio.

The current ratio, as a barometer of short-term liquidity, is limited by the nature of its components. Remember that the balance sheet is prepared as of a particular date, and the actual amount of liquid assets may vary considerably from the date on which the balance sheet is prepared. Further, as we learned from the discussion of cash flow from operations, accounts receivable and/or inventories may not be truly liquid. A firm could have a relatively high current ratio but not be able to meet demands for cash because the accounts receivable are uncollectible or the inventory is unsalable at its carrying value. Thus it is necessary to use other measures of liquidity (such as the quick ratio, the activity ratios, which rate the liquidity of specific assets, and the ability of the firm to generate cash flow from operations) to supplement the current ratio.[2]

Quick or Acid Test Ratio

$$\frac{\text{Current Assets} - \text{Inventory}}{\text{Current Liabilities}}$$

1983	1982
$\dfrac{65,846 - 47,041}{27,461} = .68 \text{ times}$	$\dfrac{56,264 - 36,769}{20,432} = .95 \text{ times}$

The quick or acid test test ratio is a more rigorous test of short-run solvency. This ratio eliminates from the numerator inventories, which are considered to be the least liquid of the current assets and the most likely source of losses. The quick ratio also indicates some deterioration of liquidity for R.E.C., Inc. at year-end 1983 compared with 1982, as current assets excluding inventory covered short-term debt only .68 times relative to .95 times. Again, this ratio must be examined in terms of the other trends and industry standards.

Activity Ratios: Liquidity of Specific Assets

Average Collection Period

$$\frac{\text{Accounts Receivable}}{\text{Average Daily Sales}}$$

1983	1982
$\dfrac{8,960}{215,600 \div 360} = \dfrac{8,960}{599} = 15 \text{ days}$	$\dfrac{8,350}{153,000 \div 360} = \dfrac{8,350}{425} = 20 \text{ days}$

The average collection period of accounts receivable is the average number of days required to convert receivables into cash. The ratio is calculated as the

---

2. For additional reading on this topic and the introduction of another liquidity ratio, see L. M. Fraser, ''Cash Flow From Operations and Liquidity Analysis, A New Financial Ratio for Commercial Lending Decisions,'' *The Journal of Commercial Bank Lending,* November, 1983.

relationship between net accounts receivable (net of the allowance for doubtful accounts) and average daily sales (sales ÷ 360 days). (Some analysts use the average balance of accounts receivable in the numerator and 365 days to determine average daily sales. Where available, the figure for "credit sales" can be substituted for net sales since it is credit sales that produce accounts receivable.) The ratio tells us that during 1983 R.E.C., Inc. collected its accounts, on average, in 15 days, which is an improvement over the 20-day collection period experienced in 1982.

The average collection period helps gauge the liquidity of accounts receivable, the ability of the firm to collect from customers. It also provides information about a company's credit policies. For instance, if the average collection period is increasing over time or is higher than the industry average, the firm's credit policies may be too lenient, and accounts receivable not sufficiently liquid. The loosening of credit could be necessary to boost sales, but at an increasing cost to the firm. On the other hand, if credit policies are too restrictive, as reflected in an average collection period that is shortening and is less than the industry average, the firm may be losing qualified customers.

The average collection period should be compared with the firm's stated credit policies. If the credit policy calls for collection within 30 days, and the average collection period is 60 days, the implication is that the company is not sufficiently stringent in its collection efforts. There could be other explanations, such as temporary problems due to a distressed economy. The analyst should attempt to determine the cause of a ratio that is too long or too short.

The analyst must also consider the strength of the firm within its industry. There are circumstances that would enable a relatively financially strong company to extend credit for longer periods than its weaker competitors.

Accounts Receivable Turnover

	1983	1982
$\dfrac{\text{Net Sales}}{\text{Accounts Receivable}}$	$\dfrac{215{,}600}{8{,}960} = 24.06$ times	$\dfrac{153{,}000}{8{,}350} = 18.32$ times

The accounts receivable turnover indicates how many times, on average, accounts receivable are collected during the year. R.E.C., Inc. converted accounts receivable into cash 24 times during 1983, up from 18 times in 1982. The turnover of receivables, like the average collection period, has improved for R.E.C., Inc. The two ratios are essentially measuring the same thing—the quality of accounts receivable and the efficiency of the firm's collection and credit policies. The turnover expresses this information in "times," while the average collection period is expressed in days. Generally, a high turnover is good because it is evidence of efficiency in converting receivables to cash, but a turnover that is too high may be indicative of credit and collection policies that are too restrictive.

Inventory Turnover

	1983	1982
$\dfrac{\text{Cost of Goods Sold}}{\text{Inventories}}$	$\dfrac{129,364}{47,041} = 2.75$ times	$\dfrac{91,879}{36,769} = 2.50$ times

Inventory turnover measures the efficiency of the firm in managing and selling inventory. It is thus a gauge of the liquidity of a firm's inventory. (The ratio is sometimes calculated with net sales in the numerator and/or with average inventory as the denominator.) The inventory turnover for R.E.C., Inc. was 2.75 times in 1983, an improvement over 2.50 times in 1982.

Generally, a high inventory turnover is a sign of efficient inventory management and profit for the firm; the faster inventory sells, the less funds are tied up in inventory. But a high turnover can also mean understocking and lost orders, a decrease in prices, a shortage of materials, or more sales than planned. A relatively low turnover could be the result of a company's carrying too much inventory or stocking inventory that is obsolete, slow-moving, or inferior. On the other hand, low turnover could stem from a stockpiling for legitimate reasons, such as increased demand or an expected strike. Obviously, the analyst should explore the cause of a turnover figure that is out of line one way or the other.

The type of industry is important in assessing inventory turnover. We would expect florists and produce retailers to have a relatively high inventory turnover because they deal in perishable products, while retailers of jewelry or farm equipment would likely have lower inventory turnover but higher profit margins. When making comparisons among firms, it is essential to check the cost flow assumption (discussed in Chapter 2) used to value inventory and cost products sold.

Fixed Asset Turnover

	1983	1982
$\dfrac{\text{Net Sales}}{\text{Net Property, Plant and Equipment}}$	$\dfrac{215,600}{29,079} = 7.41$ times	$\dfrac{153,000}{18,977} = 8.06$ times

Total Asset Turnover

	1983	1982
$\dfrac{\text{Net Sales}}{\text{Total Assets}}$	$\dfrac{215,600}{95,298} = 2.26$ times	$\dfrac{153,000}{75,909} = 2.02$ times

The fixed asset turnover and total asset turnover ratios are two approaches to assessing management's effectiveness in generating sales from investments in assets. The fixed asset turnover considers only the firm's investment in property, plant, and equipment, while the total asset turnover measures the efficiency of managing all of a firm's assets. Generally, the higher these ratios, the smaller is the investment required to generate sales and thus the more profitable is the firm. When the asset turnover ratios are low relative to the industry or the firm's historical record, either the investment in assets is too heavy and/ or sales are sluggish. Of course, there may be plausible explanations; for example, the firm may have undertaken an extensive plant modernization during the current year.

We notice that for R.E.C., Inc., the fixed asset turnover has slipped slightly between 1983 and 1982, while the total asset turnover has improved. The firm's investment in fixed assets has grown at a faster rate (53%) than sales (41%), and we will need to examine these trends in the context of our overall analysis of R.E.C., Inc.

Debt Ratio

Leverage Ratios: Debt Financing and Coverage

	1983	1982
$\dfrac{\text{Total Liabilities}}{\text{Total Assets}}$	$\dfrac{49{,}363}{95{,}298} = 51.8\%$	$\dfrac{38{,}042}{75{,}909} = 50.1\%$

Long-Term Debt to Total Capitalization

	1983	1982
$\dfrac{\text{Long-Term Debt}}{\text{Long-Term Debt + Stockholders' Equity}}$	$\dfrac{21{,}059}{21{,}059 + 45{,}935} = 31.4\%$	$\dfrac{16{,}975}{16{,}975 + 37{,}867} = 31.0\%$

Debt to Equity

	1983	1982
$\dfrac{\text{Total Liabilities}}{\text{Stockholders' Equity}}$	$\dfrac{49{,}363}{45{,}935} = 107.5\%$	$\dfrac{38{,}042}{37{,}867} = 100.5\%$

Each of the three ratios presented above measure the extent of the firm's financing with debt. The amount and proportion of debt in a company's capital structure is extemely important to the financial analyst because of the tradeoff between risk and return. Use of debt involves risk because debt carries with it a fixed commitment in the form of interest charges and principal repayment. Failure to satisfy the fixed charges associated with debt will result in bankruptcy. A lesser risk is that a firm with too much debt has difficulty in obtaining additional debt financing when needed or finds that credit is available only at extremely high rates of interest. While debt implies risk, however, it also introduces the potential for increased benefits to the firm's owners. When debt is used successfully—if operating earnings are more than sufficient to cover the fixed charges associated with debt—the returns to shareholders are magnified through financial leverage. The concept of financial leverage is illustrated on pages 119 and 120.

The debt ratio considers the proportion of all assets that are financed with debt. The ratio of long-term debt to total capitalization reveals the extent to which long-term debt is used for the firm's permanent financing (both long-term debt and equity). The debt to equity ratio measures the riskiness of the firm's capital structure in terms of the relationship between the funds supplied by creditors (debt) and investors (equity). The higher the proportion of debt, the greater is the degree of risk because creditors must be satisfied before owners in the event of bankruptcy. The equity base provides, in effect, a cushion of protection for the suppliers of debt. Each of the three ratios have increased somewhat for R.E.C., Inc. between 1982 and 1983, implying a slightly riskier capital structure.

Times Interest Earned

	1983	1982
$\dfrac{\text{Operating Profit}}{\text{Interest Expense}}$	$\dfrac{19{,}243}{2{,}585} = 7.4 \text{ times}$	$\dfrac{11{,}806}{2{,}277} = 5.2 \text{ times}$

For a firm to benefit from financial leverage (debt financing), the fixed interest payments that accompany debt must be more than satisfied from operating earnings. The more times a company can cover its annual interest expense out of operating earnings, the better off will be the firm's investors. While R.E.C., Inc. increased its use of debt between 1982 and 1983, the company also improved its ability to cover interest payments from operating profits.

Fixed Charge Coverage

	1983	1982
$\dfrac{\text{Operating Profit} + \text{Lease Payments}}{\text{Interest Expense} + \text{Lease Payments}}$	$\dfrac{19{,}243 + 13{,}058}{2{,}585 + 13{,}058} = 2.1 \text{ times}$	$\dfrac{11{,}806 + 7{,}111}{2{,}277 + 7{,}111} = 2.0 \text{ times}$

The fixed charge coverage ratio is a broader measure of a firm's coverage capabilities than the times interest earned ratio because it includes the fixed payments associated with leasing. (Lease payments are added back in the numerator because they were deducted as an operating expense to obtain operating profit.) Lease payments are similar in nature to interest expense in that they both represent obligations that must be met on an annual basis. The fixed charge coverage ratio is important for firms that operate extensively with leasing arrangements (either operating leases, used by R.E.C., Inc., or capital leases, a form of property financing described in Chapter 3). R.E.C., Inc. experienced a significant increase in the amount of annual lease payments between 1982 and 1983 but was still able to improve its fixed charge coverage slightly.

Profitability Ratios: Overall Efficiency and Performance

Gross Profit Margin

	1983	1982
$\dfrac{\text{Gross Profit}}{\text{Net Sales}}$	$\dfrac{86{,}236}{215{,}600} = 40.0\%$	$\dfrac{61{,}121}{153{,}000} = 39.9\%$

Operating Profit Margin

	1983	1982
$\dfrac{\text{Operating Profit}}{\text{Net Sales}}$	$\dfrac{19{,}243}{215{,}600} = 8.9\%$	$\dfrac{11{,}806}{153{,}000} = 7.7\%$

Net Profit Margin

	1983	1982
$\dfrac{\text{Net Earnings}}{\text{Net Sales}}$	$\dfrac{9{,}394}{215{,}600} = 4.4\%$	$\dfrac{5{,}910}{153{,}000} = 3.9\%$

These three profitability ratios are different phases of a company's ability to translate sales dollars into earnings. The gross profit margin shows the relationship between sales and the cost of products sold and thus measures the ability of a company both to control costs of inventories and to pass along price increases through sales to customers. The operating profit margin incorporates all of the expenses associated with ordinary business activities and is a measure of the overall operating efficiency of the firm. The net profit margin measures profitability after consideration of all revenue and expense, including nonoperating items and income taxes.

There was little change in R.E.C., Inc.'s gross profit margin for the years 1982 and 1983, but the company succeeded in improving its operating profit margin. Apparently R.E.C., Inc. was able to control the growth of operating expenses while sharply increasing sales. There was also a slight increase in net profit, probably resulting from the solid operating performance. It will be helpful to look at these ratios over a longer term and in conjunction with other financial data to help explain the changes.

Return on Investment (R.O.I.)

	1983	1982
$\dfrac{\text{Net Earnings}}{\text{Total Assets}}$	$\dfrac{9{,}394}{95{,}298} = 9.9\%$	$\dfrac{5{,}910}{75{,}909} = 7.8\%$

Return on Equity (R.O.E.)

	1983	1982
$\dfrac{\text{Net Earnings}}{\text{Stockholders' Equity}}$	$\dfrac{9{,}394}{45{,}935} = 20.5\%$	$\dfrac{5{,}910}{37{,}867} = 15.6\%$

Return on investment and return on equity are two ratios that measure the overall efficiency of the firm in managing its total investment in assets and in generating return to shareholders. Return on investment or return on assets indicates the amount of profit earned by a company relative to the level of investment in total assets. Return on equity, also calculated as return on common equity (if a company has preferred stock outstanding, this amount would

Figure 5.1

Summary of Financial Statement Analysis
How to Use Financial Ratios

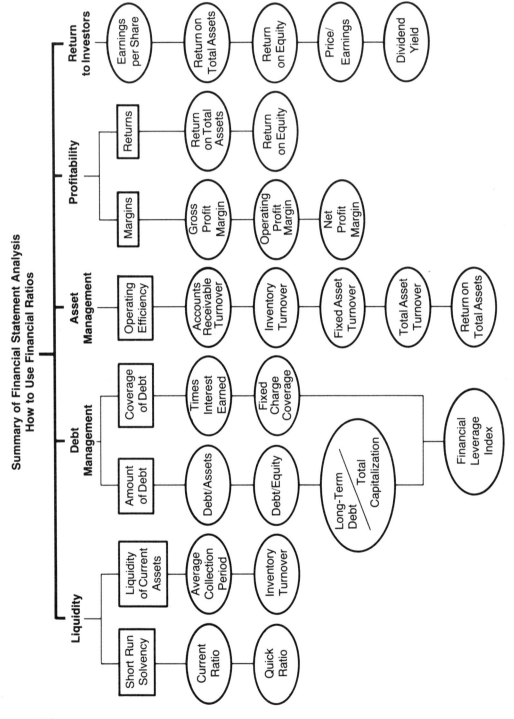

114

be subtracted from the denominator and preferred dividend payments would be deducted from the numerator), measures the return to the common shareholder. R.E.C., Inc. registered a solid improvement in 1983 relative to 1982 in terms of both return ratios.

Figure 5.1 is a summary of how to use key financial ratios. Also see Appendix E.

Would you, as a bank loan officer, extend $1.5 million in new credit to R.E.C., Inc.? Would you, as an investor, purchase R.E.C., Inc. common stock at the current market price of $30 per share? Would you, as a wholesaler of running shoes, sell your products on credit to R.E.C., Inc.? Would you, as a recent college graduate, accept a position as manager-trainee with R.E.C., Inc.? Would you, as the chief financial officer of R.E.C., Inc. open 25 new retail stores during the next two years?

THE STING

Objectives of the Analysis

In order to answer such questions we now must complete the analysis of R.E.C., Inc.'s financial statements, utilizing the common size financial statements and key financial ratios prepared in the first part of the chapter, as well as other information discussed throughout the book. It would be desirable to have an organizing theme to direct the analysis toward the goal of answering the questions raised above. The objective or perspective of the financial statement user—creditor, investor, supplier, employee, management, regulator, competitor, financial press, or other—will determine the focus of an analysis. Since we are dealing with all of the questions and with all of the financial statement group users, we will adopt a general approach covering each of the broad areas that would typically constitute a fundamental analysis of financial statements: (1) a brief descriptive section on the firm, the industry, the econ-

---

Steps of a Financial Statement Analysis

1. Establish objectives of the analysis.

2. Study industry in which firm operates and relate industry climate to current and projected economic developments.

3. Develop knowledge of firm and the quality of management.

4. Evaluate financial statements.
   - Tools: Common size financial statements, key financial ratios, trend analysis, structural analysis, and comparison with industry competitors.
   - Major Areas: Short-term liquidity, capital structure and long-term solvency, operating efficiency and profitability, market ratios, and segmental analysis (where relevant).

5. Summarize findings based upon analysis and reach conclusions about firm relevant to the established objectives.

omy, and the outlook; (2) short-term liquidity; (3) capital structure and long-term solvency; and (4) operating efficiency and profitability. It will then be necessary for the reader to select from this general coverage those areas relevant to the specific objective of a specialized analysis.

Background: Economy, Industry, and Firm

An individual company does not operate in a vacuum. Economic developments and the actions of competitors affect the ability of any business enterprise to perform successfully. It is therefore necessary to preface the evaluation of a firm's financial statements with an analysis of the environment in which the firm conducts business. This process involves blending hard facts with guesses and estimates. The analyst can be greatly helped by the sources listed on page 102. A brief section discussing the business climate of R.E.C., Inc. follows.[3]

Recreational Equipment and Clothing, Incorporated (R.E.C., Inc.) is the third largest retailer of recreational products in the U.S. The firm offers a broad line of sporting goods and equipment and active sports apparel in medium to higher price ranges. R.E.C., Inc. sells equipment used in running, basketball, golf, tennis, skiing, football, scuba diving, and other sports; merchandise for camping, hiking, fishing, and hunting; men's and women's sporting apparel; gift items; games; and consumer electronic products. The firm also sells sporting goods on a direct basis to institutional customers such as schools and athletic teams.

The general and executive officers of the company are in Dime Box, Texas, and these facilities were expanded during 1983. Most of the retail stores occupy leased spaces and are located in major regional or suburban shopping districts throughout the Sunbelt (Southeastern United States). Eighteen new retail outlets were added in late 1982, and 25 new stores were opened in 1983. The firm owns distribution center warehouses located in Alabama, Florida, Georgia, Louisiana, and Texas.

The recreational products industry is affected by current trends in consumer preferences, cyclicability with regard to sales demand, and weather conditions. Consumers have recently been adopting less expensive sports—such as running, cross-country skiing, and racquetball; while traditional and more expensive sports—golf, downhill skiing, and tennis—have experienced a decline in popularity. Recreational product retailers have been relying more heavily on sales of sportswear for their profits, since the markup on sportswear is higher than on sports equipment. With regard to seasonality, most retail sales occur in November, December, May, and June. Sales to institutions are highest in August and September. Weather conditions also influence sales volume, especially of winter sports equipment.

Competition within the recreational products industry is based on price, quality, and variety of goods offered, as well as location of outlets and quality of services. R.E.C., Inc.'s two major competitors are also full-line sporting

---

3. The background section of R.E.C., Inc. is based on a paper by Kimberly Ann Davis, "A Financial Analysis of Oshman's Sporting Goods, Inc.," March 25, 1983.

goods companies. One operates in the northwest and the other primarily in the western and southwestern United States, reducing the direct competition among the three firms.

The current outlook for the sporting goods industry is promising, following the recession in 1982. Americans have become increasingly aware of the importance of physical fitness and have become progressively more actively involved in sports. The 25 to 44 age group is the most athletically active and is projected to be the largest age group in the U.S. during the decade of the 1980s. The Sunbelt will provide a rapidly expanding market due to its fast growth in population and excellent weather conditions for year-round recreational participation.

Analysis of Financial Statements

Short-Term Liquidity

Short-term liquidity analysis is especially important to creditors, suppliers, management, and others who are concerned with the ability of a firm to meet near-term demands for cash from existing liquid resources. We already performed a portion of the analysis of R.E.C., Inc.'s short-term liquidity position through the evaluation of its common size balance sheet. We noted that inventories have increased at the expense of cash and marketable securities in the current asset section; and there has been a rise in the proportion of debt, both current and long-term. These developments were traced primarily to policies and financing needs related to new store openings. Additional evidence to contribute to the analysis of short-term liquidity is provided by a five-year trend of selected financial ratios and a comparison with industry averages for the ratios. Sources of comparative industry ratios are Dun & Bradstreet's *Key Business Ratios* (New York, N.Y.), Robert Morris Associates *Annual Statement Studies* (Philadelphia, Pa.), Standard & Poor's Corporation *Analysts Handbook* and *Industry Surveys* (New York, N.Y.), and Leo Troy's *Almanac of Business and Industrial Financial Ratios* (Prentice-Hall, Inc., Englewood Cliffs, N.J.). (In addition to or in place of these sources, the analyst can make comparisons with the same set of ratios calculated for one or more major competitors.)

R.E.C., Inc.	1983	1982	1981	1980	1979	Industry Average 1983
Current Ratio	2.40	2.75	2.26	2.68	2.83	2.53
Quick Ratio	.68	.95	.87	1.22	1.20	.97
Average Collection Period	15 days	20 days	13 days	11 days	10 days	17 days
Inventory Turnover	2.75	2.50	2.74	2.99	3.20	3.12
Cash Flow from Operations ($ Thousands) (see Ch. 4)	10,024	(3,767)	5,629	4,925	3,430	

Liquidity analysis involves an impossible task: to predict the future, the ability of the firm to meet prospective needs for cash, from the historical balance sheet valuation of liquid assets. No one financial ratio or set of financial ratios or other forms of historical financial statement data can serve as a proxy for future developments. With R.E.C., Inc. the financial ratios themselves are somewhat contradictory.

The current and quick ratios have both trended downward over the five-year period between 1979 and 1983, indicating a deterioration of short-term liquidity, and are below the industry figure for 1983. On the other side of the case, the average collection period for accounts receivable and inventory turnover ratios (after worsening between 1979 and 1982) improved in 1983. These ratios measure the quality or liquidity of accounts receivable and inventory. Average collection period rose to a high of 20 days in 1982, the recessionary year, and then fell back to a more acceptable 15-day level in 1983. This reduction of five days freed cash of $3 million, which otherwise would be tied up in receivables.[4]

The common size balance sheet of R.E.C., Inc. revealed that inventories now comprise about half of the firm's total assets. The growth in inventories has been necessary to satisfy the requirements associated with the opening of new retail outlets but has been accomplished by reducing holdings of cash and cash equivalents. This represents the tradeoff of highly liquid assets (cash and marketable securities) for potentially less liquid assets (inventories). Thus the efficient management of inventories is a critical ingredient of R.E.C., Inc.'s liquidity position. In 1983 inventory turnover improved in spite of the buildups necessary to stock new stores. Sales demand in 1983 was more than adequate to absorb the 28% increase in inventories recorded for the year.

The major question mark in the outlook for R.E.C., Inc.'s liquidity picture is the ability of the firm to produce cash flow from operations. In 1982 R.E.C., Inc. failed to generate any cash from operations, and this occurrence is certainly a threat to liquidity. The problems in 1982 stemmed from several factors. The depressed state of the economy and poor ski conditions combined to reduce sales growth. The easing of sales demand hit R.E.C., Inc. in a year that marked the beginning of a major market expansion. Inventories and receivables increased too fast for the limited sales growth of a recessionary year; R.E.C., Inc. simultaneously experienced some reduction of the credit available from

---

4. 1983 Sales $215,600,000 ÷ 360 days = $598,889 Average daily sales. $598,899 × 5 days = $2,994,445.

Another measure of liquidity is the net trade cycle or cash conversion cycle, which quantifies the amount of time (expressed in number of days) required to sell inventory and collect receivables, less credit available from suppliers. The cash conversion cycle for R.E.C., Inc. would be calculated as follows for 1983 and 1982:

	1983	1982
Accounts receivable ÷ Average daily sales	15 days	20 days
plus		
Inventory ÷ Average daily sales	79 days	87 days
less		
Accounts payable ÷ Average daily sales	(24 days)	(18 days)
Cash conversion cycle	70 days	89 days

By reducing (thus, improving) the net trade cycle by 19 days between 1982 and 1983, R.E.C., Inc. has increased cash flow by $11,378,891 (1983 average daily sales of $598,889 × 19 days).

suppliers as they felt the economic pinch. The consequence of these events was a cash crunch.

The year 1983 has seen considerable improvement, with the firm generating over $10 million in cash from operations and the progress noted earlier in the management of accounts receivable and inventories. There is no major problem with R.E.C., Inc.'s short-term liquidity position at the present time. Another poor year, however, might very well cause the same troubles experienced in 1982. The timing of any further expansion of retail outlets will be of critical importance to the on-going success of the firm.

The financial analyst should be concerned with the amount of debt in a firm's capital structure and its ability to service debt. Debt implies risk because debt involves the satisfaction of fixed financial obligations. The disadvantage of debt financing is that the fixed commitments must be met in order for the firm to continue operations. The major advantage of debt financing is that, when used successfully, shareholder returns are magnified through financial leverage. The concept of financial leverage can best be illustrated with an example.

Capital Structure and Long-Term Solvency

The Sockee Sock Company has $100,000 in total assets, and the firm's capital structure consists of 50% debt and 50% equity:

Debt	$ 50,000
Equity	50,000
Total Assets	$100,000

The cost of debt is 10%, and the company has an average tax rate of 40%. If Sockee Sock Company generates $20,000 in operating earnings, the return to shareholders, as measured by the return on equity ratio, would be 18%:

Operating earnings	$20,000
Interest expense	(5,000)
Earnings before tax	15,000
Income tax	6,000
Net earnings	$ 9,000

$$\frac{\text{Net earnings}}{\text{Equity}} = \frac{9,000}{50,000} = 18\%$$

If Sockee is able to double operating earnings to $40,000, the return on equity will more than double, increasing from 18% to 42%.

Operating earnings	$40,000
Interest expense	5,000
Earnings before tax	35,000
Tax expense	14,000
Net earnings	$21,000

$$\frac{\text{Net earnings}}{\text{Equity}} = \frac{21,000}{50,000} = 42\%$$

The magnified return on equity results from financial leverage. Interest is a fixed expense, and any funds left over after covering this fixed obligation are available to shareholders. Unfortunately, leverage has a double edge. If operating earnings at Sockee Sock Company are cut in half from $20,000 to $10,000, the return on equity is more than halved, falling from 18% to 6%.

Operating earnings	$10,000
Interest expense	5,000
Earnings before tax	5,000
Tax expense	2,000
Net earnings	$ 3,000

$$\frac{\text{Net earnings}}{\text{Equity}} = \frac{3,000}{50,000} = 6\%$$

The amount of interest expense is fixed, regardless of the level of operating earnings. When earnings decline, financial leverage produces adverse effects on shareholder returns. In evaluating a firm's capital structure and solvency, the analyst must constantly weigh the potential benefits of debt against the risks inherent in its use.

R.E.C., Inc.	1983	1982	1981	1980	1979	Industry Average 1983
Debt to Total Assets	51.8	50.1	49.2	40.8	39.7	48.7
Long-Term Debt to Total Capitalization	31.4	31.0	24.1	19.6	19.8	30.4
Debt to Equity	107.5	100.5	96.5	68.2	65.8	97.7

The above leverage ratios for R.E.C., Inc., during the 1979–1983 period reveal a steady increase in the use of borrowed funds. Total debt has risen relative to total assets, long-term debt has grown as a proportion of the firm's permanent financing, and external financing (debt) has increased relative to internal financing (equity). Given the greater degree of risk implied by borrowing, it is important for the analyst to determine (1) why debt has increased, (2) whether R.E.C., Inc. is employing financial leverage successfully, and (3) how well the firm is covering its fixed charges.

Why has debt increased? We can look to the statement of changes in financial position for an explanation of borrowing cause. Exhibits 5.4 and 5.5 present partial statements of changes in financial position showing both dollar amounts and each statement category as a percentage of total uses or sources.

Exhibit 5.4   **R.E.C., Inc.**
Partial Statement of Changes in Financial Position
For the years ended December 31, 1983, 1982, and 1981
(In thousands of dollars and (percentage) of total uses)

	1983		1982		1981	
	$	%	$	%	$	%
Uses of working capital						
Additions to property, plant and equipment	$14,100	(82.0)	$4,773	(58.0)	$3,982	(66.9)
Reductions of long-term debt	1,516	(8.8)	1,593	(19.4)	127	(2.1)
Cash dividends	1,582	(9.2)	1,862	(22.6)	1,841	(31.0)
Total Uses	$17,198	(100.0)	$8,228	(100.0)	$5,950	(100.0)

R.E.C., Inc. Exhibit 5.5
Partial Statement of Changes in Financial Position
For the years ended December 31, 1983, 1982, and 1981
(In thousands of dollars and (percentage) of total sources)

	1983		1982		1981	
	$	%	$	%	$	%
Sources of working capital						
From operations	$13,600	(68.9)	$ 9,030	(52.8)	$8,515	(91.9)
Additions to long-term debt	5,600	(28.4)	7,882	(46.1)	629	(6.8)
Sales of common stock	256	(1.3)	183	(1.1)	124	(1.3)
Other sources	295	(1.4)	—		—	
Total Sources	$19,751	(100.0)	$17,095	(100.0)	$9,268	(100.0)

R.E.C., Inc. has substantially increased its investment in fixed assets (see Exhibit 5.4), particularly in 1983 when additions to property, plant, and equipment accounted for 82% of the total uses of working capital. These investments have been financed largely from borrowing, especially in 1982 (See Exhibit 5.5) when R.E.C., Inc. had a sluggish performance record and no internal generation of cash. Operations supplied almost all of R.E.C., Inc.'s funds in 1981, but the firm had to borrow $7.9 million long-term in 1982 (46% of total sources) and $5.6 million in 1983 (28% of total sources). The impact of this borrowing was seen in the firm's leverage ratios.

How effectively is R.E.C., Inc. using financial leverage? We can find out by calculating the Financial Leverage Index (F.L.I.)[5]:

$$\frac{\text{Return on Equity}}{\text{Return on Assets (Adjusted)}}$$

When the F.L.I. is greater than 1, which indicates that Return on Equity exceeds Return on Assets, the firm is employing debt beneficially.

R.E.C., Inc.		1983	1982	1981
F.L.I.	$\dfrac{\text{Return on Equity}}{\text{Return on Assets (Adjusted)}}$	$\dfrac{20.45}{11.35} = 1.8$	$\dfrac{15.61}{9.50} = 1.6$	$\dfrac{17.53}{9.97} = 1.8$

---

5. The formula for Return on Assets in the F.L.I. is

$$\frac{\text{Net Earnings} + \text{Interest Expense} (1 - \text{Tax Rate})}{\text{Total Assets}}$$

Return on assets for R.E.C., Inc., using the F.L.I. formula would be:

1983	1982	1981
$\dfrac{9{,}394 + 2{,}585 \,(.55)}{95{,}298} = 11.35\%$	$\dfrac{5{,}910 + 2{,}277\,(.57)}{75{,}909} = 9.50\%$	$\dfrac{5{,}896 + 1{,}274\,(.55)}{66{,}146} = 9.97\%$

The average tax rate was determined as follows:

	1983	1982	1981
$\dfrac{\text{Income taxes}}{\text{Earnings before income taxes}}$	$\dfrac{7{,}686}{17{,}080} = 45.0\%$	$\dfrac{4{,}457}{10{,}367} = 43.0\%$	$\dfrac{4{,}824}{10{,}720} = 45.0\%$

The F.L.I. reveals the successful use of financial leverage by R.E.C., Inc. over the last three years, when borrowing has increased; so the firm has apparently generated operating returns sufficient to more than cover the interest payments on borrowed funds.

How well is R.E.C., Inc. covering fixed charges? Let us look now more specifically at the firm's coverage ratios:

R.E.C., Inc.	1983	1982	1981	1980	1979	Industry Average 1983
Times Interest Earned	7.44	5.18	8.84	13.34	12.60	7.2
Fixed Charge Coverage	2.09	2.01	2.27	2.98	3.07	2.5

Given the increased level of borrowing, the times interest earned ratio has declined over the five-year period but remains above the industry average. R.E.C., Inc. leases the majority of its retail outlets, so the fixed charge coverage ratio (which includes lease payments) is an important coverage measure. This ratio also has slipped, as a result of store expansion and resultant higher payments for leases and interest. Although below the industry average, the firm is still covering all fixed charges by more than two times out of operating earnings and does not at this point appear to be in any danger. It is a ratio to be monitored closely in the future, however, particularly if R.E.C., Inc. continues to expand.

Operating Efficiency and Profitability

The analysis now turns to the issues of interest to any financial statement user—a consideration of how well the firm has performed in terms of efficiency and profitability. We will begin by evaluating the trend of several key ratios.

R.E.C., Inc.	1983	1982	1981	1980	1979	Industry Average 1983
Fixed Asset Turnover	7.41	8.06	8.19	10.01	10.11	8.72
Total Asset Turnover	2.26	2.02	2.13	2.87	3.35	2.43

We noted earlier that R.E.C., Inc. has increased its investment in fixed assets as a result of home office and store expansion. The asset turnover ratios reveal a downward trend in the efficiency with which the firm is generating sales from fixed assets and total assets. The total asset turnover has improved in 1983, progress we can trace to more efficient collections of receivables and improved inventory turnover. The fixed asset turnover ratio is still falling, a result of the expansion of offices and retail outlets. If the new stores are successful, we can anticipate a turnaround in this area.

R.E.C., Inc.	1983	1982	1981	1980	1979	Industry Average 1983
Gross Profit Margin	40.00	39.95	42.00	41.80	41.76	37.25
Operating Profit Margin	8.93	7.72	8.00	11.98	12.63	7.07
Net Profit Margin	4.36	3.86	4.19	6.00	6.20	3.74

Profitability, after a relatively poor year in 1982—due to an economic recession, poor ski conditions, and the costs associated with new store openings—now looks more promising. Management adopted a growth strategy in

R.E.C. Inc.   **Exhibit 5.6**
Partial Income Statement
For the years ended 1983 and 1982
(In thousands of dollars and percent)

	$		Change 1982-1983	
	1983	1982	$	%
Net Sales	$215,600	$153,000	$62,600	40.9
Cost of goods sold	129,364	91,879	37,485	40.8
Gross Profit	86,236	61,121	25,115	41.1
Selling and administrative expenses	32,664	26,382	6,282	23.8
Advertising	14,258	10,792	3,466	32.1
Lease payments	13,058	7,111	5,947	83.6
Depreciation and amortization	3,998	2,984	1,014	34.0
Repairs and maintenance	3,015	2,046	969	47.4
Operating Profit	19,243	11,806	7,437	63.0
Interest income	422	838	(416)	(49.6)
Interest expense	(2,585)	(2,277)	(308)	(13.5)
Earnings before income taxes	17,080	10,367	6,713	64.8
Income taxes	7,686	4,457	3,229	72.4
Net Earnings	$ 9,394	$ 5,910	$ 3,484	59.0

the early 1980s with aggressive marketing and the opening of 18 new stores in 1982 and 25 in 1983. The profit margins are all below the levels recorded in 1979 and 1980 but have improved in 1983 and are above the industry averages. Although the gross profit margin has not gained ground, R.E.C., Inc. managed to improve its operating profit margin in 1983; this increase in operating profit occurred in a year with sizable increases in operating expenses, especially the lease payments required for the new stores and the repairs and maintenance of existing facilities. The net profit margin has also risen, in spite of the growth in interest payments and income tax expense and a reduction of income from marketable security investments. Exhibit 5.6 illustrates these points by showing the R.E.C., Inc. income statement for 1983 and 1982, with dollar and percentage changes.

R.E.C., Inc.	1983	1982	1981	1980	1979	Industry Average 1983
Return on Assets	9.86	7.79	8.91	10.03	10.76	10.06
Return on Equity	20.45	15.61	17.53	23.83	24.48	17.24

After declining steadily between 1979 and 1982, both return on assets and return on equity rebounded strongly in 1983. These ratios measure the overall success of the firm in generating profits from its investment and management strategies. It would appear that R.E.C., Inc. is well positioned for future growth. The analyst should keep a close watch on the firm's management of inventories, which comprise half of total assets and have caused problems in the past, and the collection period of accounts receivables. With the recent expansion of offices and stores, we would expect proportionate increases over time in repairs and maintenance expense. It is also important that the firm maintain the current level of expenditures for advertising in order to attract customers in both new and old areas. R.E.C., Inc. has financed much of its new investment with debt. Thus far, the firm has covered its fixed charges more than adequately, and its shareholders have benefited from financial leverage. With increased levels of debt, however, it is important to continue monitoring both risk and returns.

R.E.C., Inc. experienced a negative cash flow from operations in 1982, another problem that bears watching in the future. The negative cash flow occurred in a year of only modest sales growth and a decline in earnings:

R.E.C., Inc.	1983	1982	1981	1980	1979
Sales Growth	40.9%	8.7%	25.5%	21.6%	27.5%
Earnings Growth	59.0%	.2%	31.7%	28.5%	29.2%

Sales expanded rapidly in 1983 as the economy recovered and the expansion of retail outlets began to pay off. The outlook is for continued economic improvement in 1984.

Projections, Pro Formas, and Market Ratios

There are some additional analytical tools and financial ratios relevant to financial statement analysis, particularly for investment decisions and long-range planning. Although no attempt will be made to cover these topics in depth, the reader will at least be provided with an introductory treatment of projections, pro forma financial statements, and several investment-related financial ratios.

The investment analyst, in valuing securities for investment decisions, must project the future earnings stream of a business enterprise. Techniques of earnings forecasting are well beyond the scope of this book (and the author's capabilities!), but the reader is referred to two of the resources listed earlier in this chapter—Standard & Poor's *Earnings Forecaster* (Standard & Poor's Corporation, New York, N.Y.) and *The Value Line Investment Survey* (Valueline, Inc., New York, N.Y.)—as sources of earnings forecasts for individual firms.

Pro forma financial statements are projections of financial statements based on a set of assumptions regarding future revenues, expenses, level of investment in assets, financing methods and costs, and working capital management. Pro forma financial statements are utilized primarily for long-range planning and long-term credit decisions. For instance, the banker considering the extension of $1.5 million in new credit to R.E.C., Inc. could develop pro forma financial statements based on the granting of the loan, and from those statements estimate cash flow from operations in 1984 to assess the firm's coverage abilities. R.E.C., Inc.'s chief executive officer, who is making a determination regarding new store expansion, could develop pro formas based on varying estimates of performance outcomes and financing alternatives.

Four market ratios of particular interest to the investor are earnings per common share, the price/earnings ratio, the dividend payout ratio, and dividend yield. Earnings per common share is net income for the period divided by the weighted average number of common shares outstanding. One million dollars in earnings will look different to the investor if there are 1,000,000 shares of stock outstanding or 100,000 shares. The earnings per share ratio provides the investor with a common denominator to gauge the investment return.

The earnings per share computations for R.E.C., Inc. are shown below:

	1983	1982	1981
$\dfrac{\text{Net Earnings}}{\text{Average Shares Outstanding}}$	$\dfrac{9,394,000}{4,792,857} = 1.96$	$\dfrac{5,910,000}{4,581,395} = 1.29$	$\dfrac{5,896,000}{4,433,083} = 1.33$

Earnings per share appears on the income statement and was discussed in Chapter 3. R.E.C., Inc. enjoyed a large rise in earnings per share in 1983, following the decline in 1982; the price of R.E.C., Inc.'s common stock concurrently jumped from $17 at year end 1982 to $30 at the end of 1983.

The price to earnings ratio (P/E Ratio) relates earnings per common share to the market price at which the stock trades, expressing the "multiple" which the stock market places on a firm's earnings. For instance, if two competing firms had annual earnings of $2.00 per share, and Company 1 shares sold for $10.00 each while Company 2 shares were selling at $20.00 each, the market is placing a different value on the same $2.00 in earnings:

	Company 1	Company 2
$\dfrac{\text{Market Price}}{\text{Earnings per Share}}$	$\dfrac{10.00}{2.00} = 5$	$\dfrac{20.00}{2.00} = 10$

The P/E ratio or multiple for Company 2 is double that of Company 1; market investors are placing a higher valuation on the $2.00 earnings per share figure of Company 2 than of Company 1. This multiple is the function of a myriad of factors, which include future earnings potential as well as how the $2.00 per share was determined. Perhaps Company 1 has selected or changed accounting methods in order to improve earnings.

The P/E Ratio for R.E.C., Inc. would be determined as follows:

	1983	1982	1981
$\dfrac{\text{Year-End Market Price of Common Stock}}{\text{Earnings per Share}}$	$\dfrac{30.00}{1.96} = 15.3$	$\dfrac{17.00}{1.29} = 13.2$	$\dfrac{25.00}{1.33} = 18.8$

The P/E Ratio in 1983 is higher than in 1982, but below the level of 1981. This could be due to developments in the market generally and/or because the market is reacting cautiously to R.E.C., Inc.'s good year, waiting to see if improvement will continue. Another factor might be the reduction of cash dividend payments in 1983.

The dividend payout is determined by the formula cash dividends per share divided by earnings per share:

	1983	1982	1981
$\dfrac{\text{Dividends per Share}}{\text{Earnings per Share}}$	$\dfrac{.33}{1.96} = 16.8\%$	$\dfrac{.41}{1.29} = 31.8\%$	$\dfrac{.41}{1.33} = 30.8\%$

R.E.C., Inc. lowered the payment of cash dividends in 1983, producing a reduction in the dividend payout ratio. It is unusual for a company to reduce cash dividends because this move can be read as a negative signal regarding the firm's outlook. It is especially unusual to reduce cash dividends in a good year. The explanation provided by management is that the firm has adopted a new dividend policy that will result in lower dividend payments but the availability of more internal funds for reinvestment in the firm's operations. The firm plans to maintain an annual cash dividend of $.33 per share.

The dividend yield shows the relationship between cash dividends and market prices:

	1983	1982	1981
$\dfrac{\text{Dividends Per Share}}{\text{Year-End Market Price of Common Stock}}$	$\dfrac{.33}{30.00} = 1.1\%$	$\dfrac{.41}{17.00} = 2.4\%$	$\dfrac{.41}{25.00} = 1.6\%$

The R.E.C., Inc. shares are yielding a 1.1% return based on the market price at year-end 1983, down slightly from the yields in 1981 and 1982. An investor likely would choose R.E.C., Inc. as an investment more for long-term capital appreciation than for the dividend yield.

Summary of Findings

The analysis of any firm's financial statements consists of a mixture of steps and pieces that interrelate and affect each other. No one part of the analysis should be interpreted in isolation. Short-term liquidity impacts on profitability; profitability begins with sales, which relate to the liquidity of assets. The efficiency of asset management influences the cost and availability of credit that partially determine a firm's capital structure. Every aspect of a firm's financial condition and performance affects the price at which a company's securities trade in the market place.

The last step of a financial statement analysis is to integrate the pieces into a whole. The successful integration requires a summary of major findings leading to conclusions about the business enterprise. The nature of the ultimate conclusions will be relevant to the original objectives established for the analysis.

The major findings from the financial statement analysis of R.E.C., Inc. can be summarized by the following strengths and weaknesses.

Strengths

1. Favorable economic and industry outlook; R.E.C., Inc. well-positioned geographically to benefit from expected industry strength.

2. Aggressive marketing and expansion strategies.

3. Recent improvement in management of accounts receivable and inventory.

4. Successful use of financial leverage (debt) and solid coverage of debt service requirements.

5. Effective control over operating costs.

6. Substantial sales growth in 1983, partially resulting from market expansion and reflective of future performance potential.

7. Increased profitability in 1983 and generation of $10 million in cash flow from operations.

Weaknesses

1. Highly sensitive to economic fluctuations and weather conditions.

2. Negative cash flow from operations in 1982.

3. Historical problems with inventory management and some weakness in overall asset management efficiency.

4. Increased risk associated with debt financing.

The answers to specific questions regarding R.E.C., Inc. are determined by the values placed on each of the strengths and weaknesses. In general, the outlook for the firm is promising. R.E.C., Inc. appears to be a reasonably sound credit risk with attractive investment potential. The management of inventories, a continuation of effective cost controls, and careful timing of further expansion will be critically important to the future success of the firm.

THROUGH THE MAZE AND INTO THE LIGHT

The book began by describing the many intricate networks, blocked passages, and blind alleys that constitute the maze of a corporate annual report. Our objective was to navigate the maze successfully by learning how to find and interpret the information in corporate financial statements, which will lead to sound financial decisions.

In these chapters we have waded through the great volume of material found in a corporate annual report; we have dealt with the complexities and confusions created by accounting rules and choices; we have alerted ourselves to the potential for management manipulation of financial statement results; we have considered the distortions created by inflation on reported earnings and learned about ways to measure inflation's impact; we have successfully searched for information, such as cash flow from operations, which is difficult to find in a corporate annual report. Our navigation of the maze has required a close examination of the form and content of each financial statement presented in a corporate annual report and an exploration of how to analyze the statements. We have even been on a journey with Alice! It is hoped that the reader is no longer lost in the maze but is now prepared to make advantageous use of any corporate financial statements encountered in the future. The blame for any monetary losses suffered from decisions based on the content of this book will henceforth be attributed to the reader, not to the author. The author is, however, willing to take credit for any profitable results!

SELF-TEST Solutions are provided in Appendix D.

_____ 1. What is the first step in an analysis of financial statements?
(a) Check the auditor's report.
(b) Check references containing financial information.
(c) Specify the objectives of the analysis.
(d) Do a common size analysis.

_____ 2. What is a creditor's objective in performing an analysis of financial statements?
(a) To decide whether the borrower has the ability to repay interest and principal on borrowed funds.
(b) To determine the firm's capital structure.
(c) To determine the company's future earnings stream.
(d) To decide whether the firm has operated profitably in the past.

_____ 3. What is an investor's objective in financial statement analysis?
(a) To determine if the firm is risky.
(b) To determine the stability of earnings.
(c) To determine changes necessary to improve future performance.
(d) To determine whether an investment is warranted by estimating a company's future earnings stream.

_____ 4. What information does the auditor's report contain?
(a) The results of operations.
(b) An unqualified opinion.
(c) An opinion as to the fairness of the financial statements.
(d) A detailed coverage of the firm's liquidity, capital resources, and operations.

_____ 5. Which of the following would not result in a ''qualified'' auditor's report?
(a) The failure to use generally accepted accounting principles.
(b) Financial statements present fairly the financial position, results of operations, and changes in financial position.
(c) The inconsistent application of accounting principles.
(d) Uncertainties regarding the outcome of significant factors affecting the ongoing operations of the firm.

_____ 6. Which of the following is not required to be discussed in ''Management's Discussion and Analysis of the Financial Condition and Results of Operations''?
(a) Liquidity.
(b) Capital resources.
(c) Operations.
(d) Earnings projections.

7. What types of information found in supplementary schedules are required _____
   for inclusion in an annual report?
   (a) Inflation and segmental data.
   (b) Inflation data and earnings forecasts.
   (c) Material litigation and management photographs.
   (d) Management remuneration and segmental data.

8. What is Form 10-K? _____
   (a) A document filed with the AICPA, containing supplementary schedules showing management remuneration and elaborations of many financial statement disclosures.
   (b) A document filed with the Securities and Exchange Commission by
   companies selling securities to the public, containing much of the same
   information as the annual report as well as additional detail.
   (c) A document filed with the Securities and Exchange Commission containing key business ratios and forecasts of earnings.
   (d) A document filed with the Securities and Exchange Commission containing nonpublic information.

9. What information can be gained from sources such as *Key Business Ratios,* _____
   Annual Statement Studies, Analyst's Handbook, Industry Surveys and *Al-*
   manac of Business and Industrial Financial Ratios?
   (a) The general economic condition.
   (b) Forecasts of earnings.
   (c) Elaborations of financial statement disclosures.
   (d) A company's relative position within its industry.

10. Which of the following is not a tool or technique used by a financial state- _____
    ment analyst?
    (a) Common size financial statements.
    (b) Trend analysis.
    (c) Random sampling analysis.
    (d) Industry comparisons.

11. What are common size financial statements? _____
    (a) Statements that express each account on the balance sheet as a per-
    centage of total assets and each account on the income statement as a
    percentage of net sales.
    (b) Statements that standardize financial data in terms of trends.
    (c) Statements that relate the firm to the industry in which it operates.
    (d) Statements based on common sense and judgment.

12. Which of the following is not revealed on a common size balance sheet? _____
    (a) The debt structure of a firm.
    (b) The capital structure of a firm.
    (c) The dollar amount of assets and liabilities.
    (d) The distribution of assets in which funds are invested.

_____ 13. What is a serious limitation of financial ratios?
  (a) Ratios are screening devices.
  (b) Ratios can be used only by themselves.
  (c) Ratios indicate weaknesses only.
  (d) Ratios are not predictive.

_____ 14. What is the most widely used liquidity ratio?
  (a) Quick ratio.
  (b) Current ratio.
  (c) Inventory turnover.
  (d) Debt ratio.

_____ 15. What is a limitation common to both the current and the quick ratio?
  (a) Accounts receivable may not be truly liquid.
  (b) Inventories may not be truly liquid.
  (c) Marketable securities are not liquid.
  (d) Prepaid expenses are potential sources of cash.

_____ 16. Why is the quick ratio a more rigorous test of short-run solvency?
  (a) The quick ratio considers only cash and marketable securities as current assets.
  (b) The quick ratio eliminates prepaid expenses from the numerator.
  (c) The quick ratio eliminates prepaid expenses from the denominator.
  (d) The quick ratio eliminates inventories from the numerator.

_____ 17. What does an increasing collection period for accounts receivable suggest about a firm's credit policy?
  (a) The credit policy is too restrictive.
  (b) The firm is probably losing qualified customers.
  (c) The credit policy may be too lenient.
  (d) The collection period has no relationship to a firm's credit policy.

_____ 18. Which of the following statements is false about inventory turnover?
  (a) Inventory turnover measures the efficiency of the firm in managing and selling inventory.
  (b) Inventory turnover is a gauge of the liquidity of a firm's inventory.
  (c) Inventory turnover is calculated with either cost of goods sold or net sales in the numerator.
  (d) A low inventory turnover is generally a sign of efficient inventory management.

_____ 19. Which of the following is not a reason for a high inventory turnover ratio?
  (a) Stockpiling inventory.
  (b) Decrease in prices.
  (c) Understocking inventory.
  (d) Shortage of materials.

20. What do the asset turnover ratios measure for a firm? _____
    (a) The liquidity of the firm's current assets.
    (b) Management's effectiveness in generating sales from investments in assets.
    (c) The overall efficiency and profitability of the firm.
    (d) The distribution of assets in which funds are invested.

21. Which of the following ratios would not be used to measure the extent of _____ a firm's debt financing?
    (a) Debt ratio.
    (b) Debt to equity.
    (c) Times interest earned.
    (d) Long-term debt to total capitalization.

22. Why is the amount of debt in a company's capital structure important to _____ the financial analyst?
    (a) Debt implies risk.
    (b) Debt is less costly than equity.
    (c) Equity is riskier than debt.
    (d) Debt is equal to total assets.

23. Why is the fixed charge coverage ratio a broader measure of a firm's cov- _____ erage capabilities than the times interest earned ratio?
    (a) The fixed charge ratio indicates how many times the firm can cover interest payments.
    (b) The times interest earned ratio does not consider the possibility of higher interest rates.
    (c) The fixed charge ratio includes lease payments as well as interest payments.
    (d) The fixed charge ratio includes both operating and capital leases while the times interest earned ratio includes only operating leases.

24. Which profit margin measures the overall operating efficiency of the firm? _____
    (a) Gross profit margin.
    (b) Operating profit margin.
    (c) Net profit margin.
    (d) Return on equity.

25. Which ratios measure the overall efficiency of the firm in managing its _____ investment in assets and in generating return to shareholders?
    (a) Gross profit margin and net profit margin.
    (b) Return on investment.
    (c) Total asset turnover and operating profit margin.
    (d) Return on investment and return on equity.

_____ 26. What does a financial leverage index greater than "1" indicate about a firm?

(a) The unsuccessful use of financial leverage.

(b) Operating returns more than sufficient to cover interest payments on borrowed funds.

(c) More debt financing than equity financing.

(d) An increased level of borrowing.

_____ 27. What does the price to earnings ratio measure?

(a) The "multiple" which the stock market places on a firm's earnings.

(b) The relationship between dividends and market prices.

(c) The earnings for one common share of stock.

(d) The percentage of dividends paid to net earnings of the firm.

28. Match the following ratios to the corresponding calculations.

_____	(a) Current ratio	(1)	$\dfrac{\text{Accounts receivable}}{\text{Average daily sales}}$
_____	(b) Quick ratio	(2)	$\dfrac{\text{Net sales}}{\text{Net property, plant and equipment}}$
_____	(c) Average collection period	(3)	$\dfrac{\text{Total liabilities}}{\text{Total assets}}$
_____	(d) Accounts receivable turnover	(4)	$\dfrac{\text{Operating profit}}{\text{Interest expense}}$
_____	(e) Inventory turnover	(5)	$\dfrac{\text{Gross profit}}{\text{Net sales}}$
_____	(f) Fixed asset turnover	(6)	$\dfrac{\text{Current assets}}{\text{Current liabilities}}$
_____	(g) Total asset turnover	(7)	$\dfrac{\text{Net earnings}}{\text{Average shares outstanding}}$
_____	(h) Debt ratio	(8)	$\dfrac{\text{Net earnings}}{\text{Net sales}}$
_____	(i) Long-term debt to total capitalization	(9)	$\dfrac{\text{Net earnings}}{\text{Stockholders' equity}}$
_____	(j) Debt to equity	(10)	$\dfrac{\text{Cost of goods sold}}{\text{Inventories}}$
_____	(k) Times interest earned	(11)	$\dfrac{\text{Market price}}{\text{Earnings per share}}$
_____	(l) Fixed charge coverage	(12)	$\dfrac{\text{Net sales}}{\text{Total assets}}$

(m) Gross profit margin   (13) $\dfrac{\text{Long-term debt}}{\text{Long-term debt } + \text{ stockholders' equity}}$ ——

(n) Operating profit margin   (14) $\dfrac{\text{Dividends per share}}{\text{Earnings per share}}$ ——

(o) Net profit margin   (15) $\dfrac{\text{Current assets } - \text{ inventory}}{\text{Current liabilities}}$ ——

(p) Return on investment   (16) $\dfrac{\text{Operating profit } + \text{ lease payments}}{\text{Interest expense } + \text{ lease payments}}$ ——

(q) Return on equity   (17) $\dfrac{\text{Total liabilities}}{\text{Stockholders' equity}}$ ——

(r) Earnings per common share   (18) $\dfrac{\text{Net earnings}}{\text{Total assets}}$ ——

(s) Price/earnings ratio   (19) $\dfrac{\text{Net sales}}{\text{Accounts receivable}}$ ——

(t) Dividend payout ratio   (20) $\dfrac{\text{Operating profit}}{\text{Net sales}}$ ——

(u) Dividend yield   (21) $\dfrac{\text{Dividends per share}}{\text{Year-end market price of common stock}}$ ——

Use the following data to answer questions 29 through 32:

JDL Corporation
Selected Financial Data
December 31, 1983

Current assets	$150,000
Current liabilities	100,000
Inventories	50,000
Accounts receivable	40,000
Net sales	900,000
Cost of goods sold	675,000

29. JDL's current ratio is: ——
   (a) 1.0 to 1.
   (b) 0.7 to 1.
   (c) 1.5 to 1.
   (d) 2.4 to 1.

30. JDL's quick ratio is: ——
   (a) 1.0 to 1.
   (b) 0.7 to 1.
   (c) 1.5 to 1.
   (d) 2.4 to 1.

_____ 31. JDL's average collection period is:
    (a) 6 days.
    (b) 11 days.
    (c) 16 days.
    (d) 22 days.

_____ 32. JDL's inventory turnover is:
    (a) 1.25 times.
    (b) 13.5 times.
    (c) 3.0 times.
    (d) 37.5 times.

Use the following data to answer questions 33 through 35:

RQM Corporation
Selected Financial Data
December 31, 1983

Net Sales	$1,800,000
Cost of goods sold	1,080,000
Operating expenses	315,000
Net operating income	405,000
Net income	195,000
Total stockholders' equity	750,000
Total assets	1,000,000

_____ 33. RQM's gross profit margin, operating profit margin, and net profit margin respectively are:
    (a) 40.00%, 22.50%, 19.50%.
    (b) 60.00%, 19.50%, 10.83%.
    (c) 60.00%, 22.50%, 19.50%.
    (d) 40.00%, 22.50%, 10.83%.

_____ 34. RQM's return on equity is:
    (a) 26%.
    (b) 54%.
    (c) 42%.
    (d) 19%.

_____ 35. RQM's return on investment is:
    (a) 22.5%.
    (b) 26.5%.
    (c) 19.5%.
    (d) 40.5%.

Appendixes

135

How Management Can Increase Earnings Through Accounting Changes:

The Case of Union Carbide Corporation for 1980*

The Income Statement of Union Carbide Corporation and Subsidiaries for the year ended December 31, 1980, provides a dramatic example of how changes in accounting methods can increase *reported* earnings, while having no effect on cash flow or the *real* earnings potential of the firm. At the outset it should be clearly noted that the Union Carbide Corporation in 1980 did not violate any accounting or legal rules; the financial statements were prepared in accordance with generally accepted accounting principles. All accounting changes were correctly disclosed according to appropriate accounting conventions and were fully described and quantified in the notes to the financial statements. The auditor's report was unqualified other than to concur with the changes made in accounting policies.

The result of the various accounting changes, however, was to increase reported profits substantially. Union Carbide Corporation and its Subsidiaries would have reported a net income figure of $531 million for 1980 had the changes not been made; the actual profit reported was $890 million, with the difference—an increase of 68%—all due to the adoption of new accounting methods. As the company itself stated in its annual report, the changes did not affect income tax payments or cash flow. The only effect was on *reported* net income.

Exhibit A-1 shows Union Carbide's Consolidated Statement of Income and Retained Earnings for the years 1980, 1979, and 1978, just as it was published in the company's *Annual Report 1980*. "Net income" is (in millions of dollars) for years ended December 31:

	1980	1979	1978
Net Income	$890	$556	$394

It would appear that 1980 was an extremely successful year, as measured by an increase in profits of $334 million or 60% relative to 1979. This would be an outstanding performance by almost any standard. Two lines above "net

---

*A discussion of preliminary 1980 earnings for Union Carbide and the effect of its accounting changes was presented in "Union Carbide's Paper Boom," *Business Week,* February 18, 1980.

Exhibit A.1   Consolidated Statement of Income and Retained Earnings

Union Carbide Corporation and Subsidiaries	Millions of dollars (except per share figures) year ended December 31,		
	1980	1979	1978
Net sales	**$9,994**	**$9,177**	**$7,870**
Deductions (additions)			
Cost of sales	7,186	6,491	5,580
Research and development	166	161	156
Selling, administrative, and other expenses	1,152	1,053	943
Depreciation	326	470	417
Interest on long-term and short-term debt	153	161	159
Other income—net	(41)	42	(12)
Income before provision for income taxes	**1,052**	**799**	**627**
Provision for income taxes	360	251	205
Income of consolidated companies	**692**	**548**	**422**
Less: Minority stockholders' share of income	49	25	33
Plus: UCC share of income of companies carried at equity	30	33	5
Income before cumulative effect of change in accounting principle	**673**	**556**	**394**
Cumulative effect of change in accounting principle for the investment tax credit (Note 2)	217	—	—
Net income	**890**	**556**	**394**
Retained earnings at January 1*	3,486	3,120	2,905
	4,376	3,676	3,299
Dividends declared	206	190	181
Retained earnings at December 31	**$4,170**	**$3,486**	**$3,118**
Per share			
Income before cumulative effect of change in accounting principle	$10.08	$ 8.47	$ 6.09
Cumulative effect of change in accounting principle for the investment tax credit	$ 3.28	$ —	$ —
Net income†	$13.36	$ 8.47	$ 6.09
Dividends declared	$ 3.10	$ 2.90	$ 2.80
Pro forma			
Net income with 1980 change in accounting principle for the investment tax credit applied retroactively	$ 673	$ 573	$ 448
Net income per share†	$10.08	$ 8.73	$ 6.92

*After adjustment for a credit of $2.4 million in 1979 and a $0.3 million charge in 1978 for companies with which business combinations were effected on a pooling of interests basis.

†Based on 66,714,481 shares (65,673,908 shares in 1979 and 64,738,610 shares in 1978), the weighted average number of shares outstanding during the year.

The Notes to Financial Statements on pages 30 through 38 are an integral part of this statement.

Source: Union Carbide, Annual Report 1980

income,'' however, there is another set of income figures, ''Income before cumulative effect of change in accounting principle'' (in millions of dollars):

	1980	1979	1978
Income Before Cumulative Effect of Change in Accounting Principle	$673	$556	$394

Now compare 1980's profit with 1979 using these numbers, and there appears to be an increase of only $117 million, or 21%—still a hefty improvement but not as impressive as the previous measure. Which figures should be used to assess operating success? Neither, if the analyst wants to make an accurate comparison between 1979 and 1980.

Refer to Exhibit A.2, which presents the section ''Accounting Changes'' from the *Annual Report* ''Notes to Financial Statements—1980 and 1979.'' In this section Union Carbide's management explains and quantifies the various

2. ACCOUNTING CHANGES

Results for 1980 include the effects of several accounting changes adopted as of January 1, 1980. These changes, which do not affect income tax payments or cash flow, are described below.

As explained in Note 1, the flow-through method of accounting for the investment tax credit has been used rather than the deferred method. The flow-through method, which is utilized by a large majority of industry, avoids the decreasing impact of the investment tax credit that results from use of the deferred method during periods of continuing high inflation. This change in accounting principle increased 1980 net income for credits earned during the year by approximately $24 million, or $0.36 per share, which is included in the Consolidated Statement of Income and Retained Earnings as a reduction in the provision for income taxes. In addition, the cumulative effect of deferred investment tax credits for the periods through December 31, 1979, which amounted to $217 million, or $3.28 per share, has been reported as a non-recurring credit in the Consolidated Statement of Income and Retained Earnings under the caption "Cumulative effect of change in accounting principle for the investment tax credit." Pro forma net income and net income per share amounts, reflecting retroactive application of the 1980 change in method of accounting for the investment tax credit, are shown at the bottom of the income statement.

As also explained in Note 1, revised estimated useful lives have been used to depreciate the cost of machinery and equipment rather than the shorter Internal Revenue Service guideline lives adopted in 1962. The effect of this change in accounting estimate was to increase 1980 net income by approximately $94 million, or $1.41 per share.

Pursuant to Statement No. 34 of the Financial Accounting Standards Board, interest costs of $45 million in 1980 attributable to major capital projects in progress have been capitalized rather than charged to expense as incurred. The capitalized interest is being amortized over the average useful life of the assets. The effect of this change was to increase 1980 net income by approximately $24 million, or $0.36 per share.

Source: Union Carbide Annual Report 1980.

changes in accounting methods which were made in 1980. Understanding these explanations requires some knowledge of the specific accounting rules involved.

The first change relates to the accounting method used for investment tax credits, which are direct credits against income taxes that occur from fixed asset purchases by the company. Through application of an investment tax credit, a company lowers its tax payment and boosts net income. For *reporting* purposes (the financial statements published in annual reports) the company can elect one of two methods. With the flow-through method, the firm takes all of the benefit of the tax credit in the year the asset is purchased (this is also the method used for actual *tax payment* calculation); the deferred method spreads the benefit of the tax credit over the useful life of the asset that generated the credit. For example, assume that equipment with an eligible tax credit of $100,000 is purchased in 1980 and has a ten-year useful life. Under the flow-through method the company would apply the entire $100,000 as a reduction of tax expense in 1980; with the deferred method, there would be a deduction from tax expense of $10,000 per year for the years 1980–1989.

Prior to 1980 Union Carbide had used the deferred method to account for investment tax credits; in 1980 the company changed to the flow-through method. The effect of the change was twofold. Unused investment tax credits for assets purchased prior to 1980 were applied to reduce reported tax expense in 1980, thus increasing income by $217 million, or $3.28 per share (the figure shown on the income statement as the "Cumulative effect of change in accounting principle for the investment tax credit"). Use of the new method for assets purchased in 1980 increased net income (by reducing tax expense) by $24 million, or $.36 per share. There was no reduction of actual cash paid for income taxes because the credit is used in year of purchase for tax computation; thus there was no actual cash benefit from the accounting change.

The second change is a change in accounting estimate. Prior to 1980 IRS guidelines had been used to determine the depreciable lives of machinery and equipment. Effective January 1, 1980, the company began using estimates of useful life rather than IRS guidelines; the net effect was to increase the depreciation period for plant and equipment, thereby reducing annual depreciation expense and increasing net income. In 1980 net income was increased by $94 million, or $1.41 per share, as a result of this lengthening of the depreciation period.

The last adjustment is a change in an accounting principle mandated by the Financial Accounting Standards Board, the accounting organization that establishes accounting rules. FASB Statement No. 34 requires that companies capitalize the interest costs associated with certain types of assets (either self-constructed or long-term capital projects requiring progress payments), and amortize the expense over the useful life of the asset. Previously, such interest costs were expensed in the year incurred. This change increased 1980 net income $24 million, or $.36 per share.

It is interesting to note that all of the accounting changes (two optional and one required), while justified by management and approved by the auditors, served to increase net income. Had the changes not been made in 1980, Union Carbide would have experienced a decline in earnings from the previous year. For relevant comparison with 1979, the following adjustments should be made to Union Carbide's 1980 net income:

	$ Millions	$ Per Share
1980 net income as reported	$890	$13.36
1. Change from deferred to flow-through method for investment tax credits		
• Write off of I.T.C. for assets purchased prior to 1980	(217)	(3.28)
• Use of new method in 1980	(24)	(.36)
2. Lengthening of depreciation period for machinery and equipment	(94)	(1.41)
3. Capitalization of interest per FASB Statement No. 34	(24)	(.36)
1980 Net income as adjusted	$ 531	$ 7.95
1979 Net income as reported	$ 556	$ 8.47

After adjusting 1980 earnings for the accounting changes, it is evident that 1980 was a worse year than 1979 when measured by net income. An unsophisticated reader of Union Carbide's *Annual Report 1980* would probably not have made this determination.

What would be the appropriate 1980 earnings figure to use for comparison with subsequent years? The analyst should use the amount reported in Exhibit A.1 as "Income before the cumulative effect of change in accounting principle:" $673 million, or $10.08 per share. From 1980 on, the new accounting methods will be in place; and this is the income figure that incorporates those new methods and would be on an equivalent basis with future calculations of net income (assuming no other accounting changes are made!).

Accounting for Inflation **B**

In 1978 the Mythical Corporation bought a parcel of land for $500,000 and constructed a plant on the site at a cost of $1,000,000. By the end of 1982, five years later, the land was appraised at $700,000, and the cost of replacing the plant was estimated to be $1,800,000. During the five-year period, the average Consumer Price Index (C.P.I.) increased from 195.4 in 1978 to 289.1 in 1982. Question: What is the value of the Mythical Corp.'s property account (land and plant) at year-end 1982, and what amount of depreciation expense (assuming a ten-year estimated life of the plant and $0 salvage value) should be recognized in 1982? There are three sets of answers to this question, depending on the approach taken.

1. *Conventional* financial statements are based on the historical cost principle. The land and plant are recorded at original cost and carried at that amount (or, in the case of the plant, at cost less accumulated depreciation) until sold or retired from use. The value of the property account would be $1,000,000:

Property		
Land		$ 500,000
Plant	$1,000,000	
Less: Accum. Dep.	(500,000)	500,000
		$1,000,000

   Depreciation expense on the plant in 1982 would be $100,000 (cost ÷ estimated life), $1,000,000 ÷ 10 = $100,000.

2. If the value were based on *current cost,* the property account would be $1,600,000:

Property		
Land (appraisal value)		$ 700,000
Plant (replacement cost)	$1,800,000	
Less: Accum. Dep.	(900,000)	900,000
		$1,600,000

   Depreciation expense on a replacement cost basis for the plant would be $180,000 (estimated replacement cost ÷ estimated life), $1,800,000 ÷ 10 = $180,000.

3. Finally, if the amount of land and plant were determined by the increase in the *general price level*, the value of the property account would total $1,479,530:

Land	$500,000 $\times \dfrac{289.1 \text{ (1982 CPI)}}{195.4 \text{ (1978 CPI)}}$ =	$ 739,765
Plant	$1,000,000 $\times \dfrac{289.1}{195.4}$ = $1,479,530	
Less: Accum. Dep.	(739,765)	739,765
		$1,479,530

Depreciation expense in 1982 would be $147,953 (plant cost, adjusted for change in the C.P.I. ÷ estimated life),

$$\left(\$1,000,000 \times \frac{289.1}{195.4} \right) \div 10 = \$147,953.$$

To summarize, the amount in the property account on the balance sheet and depreciation expense on the income statement under each approach would be as follows:

	Property	Depreciation Expense
1. Conventional	$1,000,000	$100,000
2. Current Cost	$1,600,000	$180,000
3. General Price Level	$1,479,530	$147,953

The example of Mythical Corporation provides a simple case of the complex problems caused by inflation and the difficulties in adjusting financial statement amounts to account for inflation. The financial statements prepared on a conventional basis do not render a realistic valuation of property or measurement of the expense associated with the property when price increases are considered. But how should the amounts be adjusted? It is obvious that price movements for specific assets do not usually change at exactly the same rate as general inflation. Between 1978 and 1982 the general price level (as measured by the C.P.I.) increased by about 50%; Mythical Corp.'s land rose in value by 40%, and the replacement cost of its plant jumped by 80%. If Mythical Corp. had purchased equipment during each of the five years, every purchase would have been made with dollars of different amounts of purchasing power; any inflation adjustments for changes in the *general price level* would have to account for these differences, while adjustments made for the *current cost* of equipment would have to consider the specific changes in the price of each item purchased.

To generalize, the balance sheet fixed asset accounts for most U.S. firms are understated because prices have risen since the assets were purchased and recorded. Depreciation expense is also understated because depreciation is a cost allocation based on the undervalued historical cost of fixed assets. The effect of inflation on inventory and cost of goods sold, the other major categories of potential inflationary impact, depends on the cost flow assumption used to value inventory (see Chapter 2). During a period of inflation a LIFO company would have undervalued inventory and currently valued cost of goods sold expense, while use of FIFO produces an understated cost of goods sold and currently valued inventory. During a period of inflation, the net result—of understated depreciation expense for most firms and understated cost of goods sold for companies that do not use LIFO—is an *overstatement of net income* in the earnings statements of most U.S. companies.

The impact of inflation is uneven. For capital intensive industries with outdated plant and equipment—such as steel, autos, and paper—the toll taken by inflation has been tremendous. On the other hand, some industries—such as electronics, instruments, and computers—have been virtually unscathed by inflation.

The accounting rule-writers wrestled for many years with the challenge of how to account for inflation. Reliance on historical cost renders statements that are objective and verifiable but, in many cases, meaningless. If the relevant accounts are adjusted for inflation, however, there is controversy over how the adjustments should be made. The *general price level* (also called the *constant dollar*) approach adjusts each account by applying the change in a general price index, such as the C.P.I. or the G.N.P. deflator, to the historical cost of the asset. The *current cost* approach considers the specific price change of each asset. Since the general price level method is still based on historical cost, it is considered to be more objective, and it is also less costly and easier to apply because one index is used for all assets. On the other hand, current cost is probably more relevant and useful for analysts, but it is also a more subjective and costly approach, requiring estimates of the current value of each individual asset.[1]

In October, 1979 the Financial Accounting Standards Board issued Statement of Financial Accounting Standards Number 33, ''Financial Reporting and Changing Prices,'' which requires large,[2] publicly traded companies to disclose supplementary schedules to account for the impact of inflation on key balance sheet items—specifically inventory and property, plant, and equipment—and their related income statement expenses—cost of goods sold and depreciation. Income from continuing operations is recalculated to account for inflation-adjusted expenses. Note that these data are *supplementary* to the primary financial statements, which are still prepared on a conventional, historical cost basis. Also, the inflation accounting data are unaudited.

The accounting authorities, for at least a five-year trial period, could not decide between the two different approaches to accounting for inflation and therefore adopted both. Thus, the inflation section is presented in dual format showing both constant dollar and current cost adjustments. For the F.A.S.B.

---

1. For background reading on the issuance of Statement of Financial Accounting Standards Number 33 and the pros and cons of the constant dollar and current cost approaches, see ''Inflation Accounting,'' *Business Week,* October 15, 1979.

2. $1 billion of total assets or $125 million of inventories and gross property, plant, and equipment.

Exhibit B.1

Browning-Ferris Industries, Inc. and Subsidiaries

Notes to Financial Statements—(Continued)
Statement of Income Adjusted for Changing Prices
For the Year Ended September 30, 1982
(In Thousands)

	As Reported in the Primary Statements	Adjusted for General Inflation Constant Dollars	Adjusted for Changes in Current Costs
Revenues	$714,945	$714,945	$714,945
Costs and expenses excluding depreciation expense	525,876	525,876	525,876
Depreciation expense	67,190	85,456	89,525
Interest, net	5,811	5,811	5,811
Income before income taxes	116,068	97,802	93,733
Income taxes	53,391	53,391	53,391
Net income	$ 62,677	$ 44,411	$ 40,342
Gain from decline in purchasing power of net amounts owed		$ 4,632	$ 4,632
Effect of increase in general price level			$ 21,902
Increase in specific current cost of property and equipment held during the year*			8,360
Excess of increase in general price level over increase in the current cost			$ 13,542

*At September 30, 1982, the current cost of property and equipment, net of accumulated depreciation was $482,415.

Source: Browning-Ferris Industries, Inc. Annual Report 1982.

disclosures, companies use the C.P.I. to account for general price level changes (constant dollar) and are allowed a variety of techniques—direct pricing, external price indexes, internally generated price indexes—to determine specific price changes (current cost).

In addition to the income statement disclosures, companies are required to present a five-year summary of data showing revalued net assets at year-end, per share amounts of income from continuing operations, net sales and other operating revenues, cash dividends per share, the market price per share at year-end, and the average consumer price index.

Browning-Ferris Industries, Inc. and Subsidiaries

Notes to Financial Statements—(Continued)
Five-Year Comparison of Selected Financial Data
Adjusted for Effects of Changing Prices
(In Average 1982 Fiscal Year Dollars)
(In Thousands Except for Per Share Amounts)

	Year Ended September 30,				
	1982	1981	1980	1979	1978
Revenues					
As reported	$714,945	$660,670	$552,854	$457,086	$362,888
In constant 1982 dollars	$714,945	$709,560	$659,555	$619,351	$542,518
Historical cost					
information adjusted					
for general inflation					
Net income	$ 44,411	$ 37,397	$ 19,107		
Earnings per common share	$ 1.46	$ 1.27	$ .68		
Net assets at year end	$399,597	$387,894	$357,899		
Current cost information					
Net income	$ 40,342	$ 40,201	$ 16,800		
Earnings per common share	$ 1.33	$ 1.36	$ .60		
Excess of increase in general price					
level over increase in					
current cost	$ 13,542	$ 21,558	$ 17,127		
Net assets at year end	$407,278	$388,280	$361,067		
Gain from decline in					
purchasing power of					
net amounts owed	$ 4,632	$ 12,609	$ 17,316		
Cash dividends declared					
per common share					
As reported	$ .67	$ .56	$ .47	$ .40	$ .33
In constant 1982 dollars	$ .67	$ .60	$ .56	$ .54	$ .50
Market price per common					
share at year end					
In historical dollars	$ 24.58	$ 18.17	$ 15.67	$ 9.50	$ 9.67
In constant 1982 dollars	$ 24.58	$ 19.51	$ 18.69	$ 12.87	$ 14.45
Average consumer price index	286.0	266.2	239.7	211.0	191.3

Source: Browning-Ferris Industries, Inc. Annual Report 1982.

Exhibits B.1 and B.2 illustrate the 1982 supplementary inflation schedules for Browning-Ferris Industries, Inc., a waste collection and processing firm. Refer first to Exhibit B.1, which contains the income statement adjustments. The first column shows revenues and expenses as reported in the primary statements of the annual report; the second and third columns are the same data, reflecting the effect of price changes. Revenues and expenses, other than depreciation, are already stated in average 1982 dollars. Depreciation expense is revised upward when adjusted for both general inflation and current costs, and the result is a reduced net income figure.

Note that net earnings *are* adjusted for inflation, while income taxes *are not*; some companies use this disclosure as an argument for tax relief because of the upward effect on the average tax rate:

	As Reported in the Primary Statements	Adjusted for General Inflation Constant Dollars	Adjusted for Changes in Current Costs
$\dfrac{\text{Income taxes}}{\text{Income before income taxes}}$	$\dfrac{53,391}{116,068} = 46.0\%$	$\dfrac{53,391}{97,802} = 54.6\%$	$\dfrac{53,391}{93,733} = 57.0\%$

The line below net income shows the "Gain from decline in purchasing power of net amounts owed." When a firm has debt outstanding, and the purchasing power of the dollar decreases in value due to inflation, the debt will be repaid in "cheaper" dollars. The gain for Browning-Ferris results from its net monetary liability position.[3] The remaining three lines of Exhibit B.1 isolate the difference between the increase in the general price level and the increase in specific prices of property and equipment held during the year.

Exhibit B.2 presents the required inflation accounting data for five years. Some items are reported for only three years because the effective date for compliance with FASB Statement Number 33 was for fiscal years ended on or after December 25, 1979. By 1984 the summary data will be complete for Browning-Ferris, Inc. The five-year summary data afford an opportunity to compare *nominal* (reported) changes in items such as revenue and cash dividends with real (inflation adjusted) growth. The increase in revenues and dividends for Browning-Ferris between 1978 and 1982 are shown below:

1978–1982	$Increase (thousands)	% Increase
Revenues—as reported	$352,057	97%
—in constant $	$172,427	32%
Dividends—as reported	$ .34	103%
—in constant $	$ .17	34%

The apparent growth in revenues (97%) and cash dividends (103%) for Browning-Ferris is greatly reduced to 32% and 34%, respectively, when measured in real, as opposed to nominal, terms.

Many firms have been more drastically affected by the inflation disclosures than demonstrated by the Browning-Ferris example. For some companies, profit turns to loss when earnings are adjusted for inflation. Exhibit B.3, the "Schedule of Income Adjusted for Changing Prices" from the *General Motors Annual Report 1981*, furnishes such an illustration. Reported *profit,* as recorded

---

3. A purchasing power loss would occur for firms in a net monetary asset position. "Monetary" assets and liabilities are items (such as cash, marketable securities, accounts receivable, and all liabilities other than deferred income to provide goods or services) which are stated in terms of current value and do not have to be adjusted for inflation.

SCHEDULE B

Schedule of Income Adjusted for Changing Prices
For The Year Ended December 31, 1981
(Dollars in Millions Except Per Share Amounts)

	As Reported in the Financial Statements (Historical Cost)	Adjusted for General Inflation (1981 Constant Dollar)	Adjusted for Changes in Specific Prices (1981 Current Cost)
Net Sales	$62,698.5	$62,698.5	$62,698.5
Cost of sales	55,185.2	55,766.5	55,413.5
Depreciation and amortization expense	4,406.2	4,991.6	5,200.1
Other operating and nonoperating items—net	2,896.8	2,896.8	2,896.8
United States and other income taxes (credit)	(123.1)	(123.1)	(123.1)
Total costs and expenses	62,365.1	63,531.8	63,387.3
Net Income (Loss)	$ 333.4	($ 833.3)(A)	($ 688.8)(A)
Earnings (Loss) per share of common stock	$1.07	($2.83)(A)	($2.35)(A)
Unrealized gain from decline in purchasing power of dollars of net amounts owed		$ 657.3	$ 657.3
Excess of increase in general price level over increase in specific prices of inventory and property			$ 1,686.2 (B)

Source: General Motors Annual Report 1981.

in the primary financial statements on a historical cost basis for the year ended December 31, 1981, was $333.4 billion. When adjusted for the effects of general inflation, GM experienced a *loss* of $833.3 million. The firm fared slightly better under the current cost approach, with a *loss* of $688.8 million. This difference between constant dollar and current cost is explained by the adjustments to cost of sales and depreciation. The adjustment to cost of goods sold expense was $353 million *less* ($55,766.5 − $55,413.5) on a current cost than a constant dollar basis; the depreciation expense adjustment was $208.5 million *greater* ($5200.1 − $4991.6) under current cost. This means that the prices of inventories increased slower than the rate of general inflation, but fixed asset costs grew at a more rapid pace. Regardless of the method used, General Motors' reported earnings suffer considerably when the impact of inflation is considered.

The new inflation requirements are viewed by the accounting profession as experimental in nature, not as a final answer. It is clearly important that the financial statement analyst be aware of the distortions caused by inflation. The supplementary inflation accounting data provide at least partial help in measuring the degree of distortion and its effect on profit measurement.

The Analysis of Segmental Data

Diversified companies that operate in different industries are required by the provisions of Statement of Financial Accounting Standards Number 14, "Financial Reporting for Segments of a Business Enterprise," to disclose supplementary financial data for each reportable segment. F.A.S.B. Statement Number 14 also covers reporting requirements for foreign operations, export sales, and sales to major customers. Segmental disclosures are valuable to the financial analyst in identifying areas of strength and weakness within a company; proportionate contribution to revenue and profit by each division; the relationship between capital expenditures and rates of return for operating areas; and segments that should be de-emphasized or eliminated. The information on segments is presented as a supplementary section in the notes to the financial statements, as part of the basic financial statements, or in a separate schedule that is referenced to and incorporated into the financial statements.

An *industry segment* is defined by F.A.S.B. Statement Number 14 as a component of a business enterprise that sells primarily to outside markets and for which information about revenue and profit is accumulated. *Segment revenue* includes sales of products and services to unaffiliated customers and intersegment sales, with company transfer prices used to determine sales between segments. *Operating profit or loss* is segment revenue less all operating expenses. *Segment operating expense* includes expenses relating to unaffiliated customers and segment revenue; expenses not directly traceable to segments are allocated to segments on a reasonable basis. Operating expenses *exclude* general corporate revenue and expenses, income taxes, extraordinary items, and interest expense. *Identifiable assets* are tangible and intangible assets associated with or used by a segment and include an allocated portion of jointly used assets.[1]

A segment is considered to be reportable if any one of three criteria is met:

1. Revenue is 10% or more of combined revenue, including intersegment revenue.

2. Operating profit or loss is 10% or more of the greater of combined profit of all segments with profit or combined loss of all segments with loss.

---

1. P. D. Delaney and I.N. Gleim, Outline of SFAS 14, 1983 Edition *CPA Examination Review*. (New York: John Wiley & Sons, Inc., 1983).

3. Identifiable assets exceed 10% or more of combined identifiable assets of all segments.

The following information is to be presented for each reportable segment and in the aggregate for remaining segments not reported separately:

1. Segment revenue

2. Operating profit (loss)

3. Carrying amount of identifiable assets

4. Aggregate depreciation, depletion, and amortization

5. Capital expenditures.

Exhibits C.1 and C.2 illustrate the segmental disclosures for AMF Incorporated from the 1982 annual report. AMF has seven reportable segments: Automated Process Equipment, Electronic Controls and Systems, Energy Services and Products, Specialty Materials, Bowling Products, Marine Products, and Sports Products. Segmental reporting does not include complete financial statements, but it is feasible to perform an analysis of the key financial data presented.

Exhibit C.1   **Revenue and Operating Profit by**   AMF Incorporated
Product Category (Continuing Operations)
(in thousands of dollars)

	1982	1981	1980
Revenue			
Automated Process Equipment	$ 114,805	$ 113,160	$ 137,377
Electronic Controls & Systems	165,132	189,390	191,448
Energy Services & Products	286,223	306,704	200,521
Specialty Materials	69,937	82,048	74,356
Total Industrial Technology	**636,097**	691,302	603,702
Bowling Products	155,577	158,610	145,426
Marine Products	64,755	88,967	69,452
Sports Products	197,789	212,925	231,202
Total Leisure Products	**418,121**	460,502	446,080
Total Revenue	**$1,054,218**	$1,151,804	$1,049,782
Operating Profit			
Automated Process Equipment	$ 14,569	$ 18,680	$ 20,399
Electronic Controls & Systems	10,655	15,435	16,341
Energy Services & Products	40,166	63,181	39,699
Specialty Materials	6,913	16,553	13,703
Total Industrial Technology	**72,303**	113,849	90,142
Bowling Products	39,043	44,699	42,460
Marine Products	(4,737)	4,784	2,478
Sports Products	8,678	18,703	16,328
Total Leisure Products	**42,984**	68,186	61,266
Product Category Totals	115,287	182,035	151,408
Corporate Expenses	(59,889)	(65,882)	(69,347)
Income Before Income Taxes	$ 55,398	$ 116,153	$ 82,061

Sales between product categories are insignificant and have been eliminated in arriving at total revenue. Operating profit is total revenue less cost of sales and expenses (excluding corporate expenses) plus interest and other income to the extent specifically related to product categories.

Source: AMF Incorporated Annual Report, 1982.

Refer first to Exhibit C.1. 1982 has been a generally poor year for AMF Incorporated with total revenue declining by 8% and operating profit falling by 52%. Revenue decreased for every segment except Automated Process Equipment, which was salvaged by a record performance by AMF Legg (the tobacco equipment manufacturing subsidiary in the United Kingdom). Profit was lower in 1982 for all seven segments.

In order to analyze the performance for each segment, several tables have been prepared from computations based on the figures provided in Exhibits C.1 and C.2. Table C.1 shows the percentage contribution to total revenue by segment.

Note the change in trends over the three-year period. In 1980 the major producer of revenue was Sports Products; by 1982 Energy Services and Products was clearly dominant, increasing revenue share from 19% to 27%. Energy

Product Categories   AMF Incorporated   **Exhibit C.2**

The Company's operations are included in seven principal product categories. Automated Process Equipment includes labor saving machinery for industrial use by the apparel, bakery, food, food service, tire and tobacco industries. Electronic Controls & Systems include relays, switches, timing devices, controls, control systems, circuit breakers and motors. Energy Services & Products are electronic inspection and coating services for oil field tubulars, directional drilling instruments and services, and instruments to obtain seismic data, while Specialty Materials include liquid filtration, and medical diagnostic products. Bowling Products include automatic pinspotters and scoring systems, lanes, bowling balls, pins, bags and shoes, while Marine Products include yachts and sailboats. Sports Products include sporting goods equipment used for golf, tennis and other racquet sports, snow skiing and various team sports.

Assets, Depreciation & Capital Expenditures
(in thousands of dollars)

	Identifiable Assets			Depreciation & Amortization			Capital Expenditures		
	1982	1981	1980	1982	1981	1980	1982	1981	1980
Automated Process Equipment	$ 57,076	$ 63,635	$ 82,439	$ 3,540	$ 3,616	$ 3,358	$ 5,556	$ 3,899	$ 3,509
Electronic Controls & Systems	84,802	96,476	98,899	5,795	5,187	4,099	8,343	7,683	10,010
Energy Services & Products	286,450	255,690	148,359	24,686	17,120	11,869	84,060	83,531	41,554
Specialty Materials	52,777	55,025	50,434	3,102	2,834	2,458	3,702	6,495	6,832
Total Industrial Technology	481,105	470,826	380,131	37,123	28,757	21,784	101,661	101,608	61,905
Bowling Products	150,357	168,046	170,354	5,333	6,111	6,795	7,724	7,181	7,310
Marine Products	41,678	41,528	38,009	2,234	2,201	1,849	4,211	2,902	3,936
Sports Products	123,059	124,438	135,583	4,985	4,952	5,028	5,971	6,583	6,507
Total Leisure Products	315,094	334,012	343,946	12,552	13,264	13,672	17,906	16,666	17,753
Product Category Totals	796,199	804,838	724,077	49,675	42,021	35,456	119,567	118,274	79,658
Corporate amounts.....	93,870	86,706	69,492	1,568	2,283	1,768	1,176	1,052	671
Total Continuing Operations	890,069	891,544	793,569	$51,243	$44,304	$37,224	$120,743	$119,326	$80,329
Net Assets of Discontinued Operations	—	39,827	136,470						
Total Assets	$890,069	$931,371	$930,039						

Identifiable assets include both assets directly related to product categories and an allocable share of jointly used assets. Corporate assets consist primarily of cash and short term investments, future income tax benefits and corporate administrative facilities. Capital expenditures include additions to machines leased to customers.

Source: AMF Incorporated Annual Report, 1982.

Table C.1

	(Percentages)		
	1982	1981	1980
Contribution by segment to revenue:			
Automated Process Equipment	10.89	9.83	13.09
Electronic Controls and Systems	15.66	16.44	18.24
Energy Services and Products	27.15	26.63	19.10
Specialty Materials	6.64	7.12	7.08
Bowling Products	14.76	13.77	13.85
Marine Products	6.14	7.72	6.62
Sports Products	18.76	18.49	22.02
Total Revenue	100%	100%	100%

Table C.2

	(Percentages)		
	1982	1981	1980
Contribution by segment to operating income:			
Automated Process Equipment	12.64	10.26	13.47
Electronic Controls and Systems	9.24	8.48	10.79
Energy Services and Products	34.84	34.71	26.22
Specialty Materials	5.99	9.09	9.05
Bowling Products	33.87	24.56	28.04
Marine Products	(4.11)	2.63	1.64
Sports Products	7.53	10.27	10.79
Total Operating Profit	100%	100%	100%

Services and Products are operations related to oil field service activities, while Sports Products include sporting goods equipment used for golf, racquet sports, snow skiing, and team sports. Electronic Controls and Equipment remains the third largest contributor to revenue at 15.7%. Bowling products, long associated with the AMF name, generated 14.8% of AMF's total revenue in 1982, followed by Automated Process Equipment (industrial machinery), Specialty Materials (liquid filtration and medical diagnostic products) and Marine Products (yachts and sailboats).

Table C.2 reveals the contribution by segment to operating income and provides a basis for assessing the ability of a segment to translate revenue into profit.

Energy Products and Services was the leading contributor to operating profit in 1982 at 35%; Bowling Products was a very close second at 34%, up from a 28% share in 1980. Sports Products, which was ranked No. 2 in terms of revenue in 1982, fell way behind in profit contribution, with a 7.5% share. Marine Products registered an operating loss.

Operating Profit Margin (operating profit divided by revenue) is presented for each segment in Table C.3.

The operating profit margin shows the percent of every sales dollar that is converted to (before-tax) profit. The profit margin is highest in 1982 for Bowling Products, with Energy Services and Products second, and Automated Process Equipment third. Operating profit margins declined for all seven segments between 1981 and 1982 and were especially sharp for the Specialty Materials and Marine Products segments.

Table C.4 is a percentage breakdown of capital expenditures by segment.

Table C.3

	(Percentages)		
	1982	1981	1980
Operating Profit Margin by Segment:			
Automated Process Equipment	12.69	16.51	14.85
Electronic Controls and Systems	6.45	8.15	8.54
Energy Services and Products	14.03	20.60	19.80
Specialty Materials	9.88	20.17	18.43
Bowling Products	25.10	28.18	29.20
Marine Products	(7.32)	5.38	3.57
Sports Products	4.39	8.78	7.06

Table C.4

	(Percentages)		
	1982	1981	1980
Capital Expenditures by Segments:			
Automated Process Equipment	4.65	3.30	4.40
Electronic Controls and Systems	6.98	6.50	12.56
Energy Services and Products	70.30	70.62	52.17
Specialty Materials	3.10	5.49	8.58
Bowling Products	6.46	6.07	9.18
Marine Products	3.52	2.45	4.94
Sports Products	4.99	5.57	8.17
Total Capital Expenditures	100%	100%	100%

Table C.5

	(Percentages)		
	1982	1981	1980
Return on Investment by Segment:			
Automated Process Equipment	25.53	29.35	24.74
Electronic Controls and Systems	12.56	16.00	16.52
Energy Services and Products	14.02	24.71	26.76
Specialty Materials	13.10	30.08	27.17
Bowling Products	25.97	26.60	24.92
Marine Products	(11.37)	11.52	6.52
Sports Products	7.05	15.03	12.04

It is obvious that the firm's management has elected to invest heavily in Energy Services and Products, with very minimal expenditures elsewhere among the segments. Notice also in Exhibit C.2 that in 1980 Bowling Products was the largest segment, as measured by total Identifiable Assets. By 1982 Energy Services and Products had almost doubled in size and is now the dominant segment, with Bowling Products second and Sports Products third.

It is important to examine the relationship between investment and return, and this information is provided in Table C.5, which shows Return on Investment by segment (operating profit divided by identifiable assets).

Bowling Products and Automated Process Equipment have consistently generated the highest returns. The return on assets fell off sharply in 1982 for Energy Services and Products, Specialty Materials, and Marine Products.

While Energy Services and Products contributes the highest percentage of operating profit (35%), the deterioration of operating profit margin and return

Table C.6

1982	Percentage of Total Identifiable Assets	Percent Contribution to Operating Income	Operating Profit Margin	Return on Investment
Energy Services and Products	36.0	34.8	14.0	14.0
Bowling Products	18.9	33.9	25.1	26.0
Sports Products	15.5	7.5	4.4	7.1
Electronic Controls and Systems	10.6	9.2	6.5	12.6
Automated Process Equipment	7.2	12.6	12.7	25.5
Specialty Materials	6.6	6.0	9.9	13.1
Marine Products	5.2	(4.1)	(7.3)	(11.4)

on investment are alarming developments (although not surprising in view of the general slump in energy during 1982). Clearly the Marine Products division is in trouble, with negative returns in 1982. This is an area in which the firm has been increasing investment. Management blamed softness in the boating industry for the decreased 1982 revenue.

Table C.6 compares a ranking of segments in 1982 by identifiable assets with percentage contribution to operating income, operating profit margin, and return on investment.

Overall, Bowling Products and Automated Process Equipment appear to be the strongest segments and have also performed consistently well over the three-year period. Problem divisions are apparently Marine Products and, to a lesser extent, Sports Products. Given the large doses of capital investment in Energy Services and Products, and the recent decline in that segment's return ratios, it is another division that requires close scrutiny in the future.

Summary The analytical tools used to assess the segmental data of AMF Incorporated are applicable to the segmental disclosures for any company. Minor variations and/or additions to the set of tables prepared for AMF Incorporated may be appropriate for a particular company, but the basic analysis should include, by segment and for at least a three-year period: (1) percentage contribution to revenue, (2) percentage contribution to operating income, (3) operating profit margin, (4) capital expenditures, (5) return on investment, and (6) an examination of the relationship between the size of a division and its relative contribution.

Solutions to Self-Tests **D**

Chapter 2

1. (b)	16. (a)	(h) C	(l) 2
2. (a)	17. (c)	(i) NC	(m) 1
3. (b)	18. (b)	(j) NC	(n) 6
4. (c)	19. (b)	24. (a) 4	(0) 8
5. (b)	20. (d)	(b) 5	25. (a) 7
6. (a)	21. (d)	(c) 8	(b) 1
7. (d)	22. (c)	(d) 7	(c) 5
8. (c)	23. (a) NC	(e) 1	(d) 9
9. (b)	(b) C	(f) 2	(e) 4
10. (c)	(c) C	(g) 2	(f) 6
11. (d)	(d) C	(h) 5	(g) 10
12. (a)	(e) NC	(i) 8	(h) 2
13. (c)	(f) C	(j) 5	(i) 3
14. (b)	(g) C	(k) 3	(j) 8
15. (d)			

Chapter 3

1. (c)	12. (a)	(e) 5	(2) d
2. (b)	13. (a)	(f) 14	(3) a
3. (a)	14. (c)	(g) 1	(4) c
4. (c)	15. (d)	(h) 6	(5) d
5. (d)	16. (c)	(i) 11	(6) a
6. (a)	17. (b)	(j) 2	(7) e
7. (c)	18. (a)	(k) 10	(8) c
8. (d)	19. (a) 4	(l) 12	(9) c
9. (d)	(b) 9	(m) 3	(10) b
10. (b)	(c) 13	(n) 7	(11) d
11. (b)	(d) 8	20. (1) c	(12) c **157**

Chapter 4

1. (c)	14. (d)	(e) U	(g) O
2. (d)	15. (a)	(f) U	(h) N
3. (b)	16. (a)	(g) S	(i) O
4. (a)	17. (b)	(h) N	(j) N
5. (c)	18. (d)	(i) S	25. (a) A
6. (b)	19. (a)	(j) U	(b) S
7. (a)	20. (b)	24. (a) O	(c) S
8. (c)	21. (c)	(b) N	(d) A
9. (d)	22. (b)	(c) O	(e) S
10. (d)	23. (a) U	(d) N	26. (a)
11. (b)	(b) S	(e) O	27. (c)
12. (b)	(c) N	(f) N	28. (a)
13. (c)	(d) S		

Chapter 5

1. (c)	15. (a)	(b) 15	(p) 18
2. (a)	16. (d)	(c) 1	(q) 9
3. (d)	17. (c)	(d) 19	(r) 7
4. (c)	18. (d)	(e) 10	(s) 11
5. (b)	19. (a)	(f) 2	(t) 14
6. (d)	20. (b)	(g) 12	(u) 21
7. (a)	21. (c)	(h) 3	29. (c)
8. (b)	22. (a)	(i) 13	30. (a)
9. (d)	23. (c)	(j) 17	31. (c)
10. (c)	24. (b)	(k) 4	32. (b)
11. (a)	25. (d)	(l) 16	33. (d)
12. (c)	26. (b)	(m) 5	34. (a)
13. (d)	27. (a)	(n) 20	35. (c)
14. (b)	28. (a) 6	(o) 8	

Summary of Financial Ratios

Ratio	Method of Computation	Significance
Current ratio	$\dfrac{\text{Current assets}}{\text{Current liabilities}}$	Measures short-term liquidity, the ability of a firm to meet needs for cash as they arise.
Quick or Acid-test ratio	$\dfrac{\text{Current assets} - \text{inventory}}{\text{Current liabilities}}$	Measures short-term liquidity more rigorously than the current ratio by eliminating inventory, generally the least liquid current asset.
Average collection period	$\dfrac{\text{Accounts receivable}}{\text{Average daily sales}}$	Indicates days required to convert receivables into cash.
Accounts receivable turnover	$\dfrac{\text{Net sales}}{\text{Accounts receivable}}$	Indicates how many times receivables are collected during a year.
Inventory turnover	$\dfrac{\text{Cost of goods sold}}{\text{Inventories}}$	Measures efficiency of the firm in managing and selling inventory.
Fixed asset turnover	$\dfrac{\text{Net sales}}{\text{Net property, plant and equipment}}$	Measures efficiency of the firm in managing fixed assets.
Total asset turnover	$\dfrac{\text{Net sales}}{\text{Total assets}}$	Measures efficiency of the firm in managing all assets.
Debt ratio	$\dfrac{\text{Total liabilities}}{\text{Total assets}}$	Shows proportion of all assets that are financed with debt
Long-term debt to total capitalization	$\dfrac{\text{Long-term debt}}{\text{Long-term debt} + \text{stockholders' equity}}$	Measures the extent to which long-term debt is used for permanent financing.
Debt to equity	$\dfrac{\text{Total liabilities}}{\text{Stockholders' equity}}$	Measures the relative proportion of funds provided by creditors (debt) and owners (stockholders' equity).
Times interest earned	$\dfrac{\text{Operating profit}}{\text{Interest expense}}$	Measures how many times interest expense is covered by operating earnings.
Fixed charge coverage	$\dfrac{\text{Operating profit} + \text{lease payments}}{\text{Interest expense} + \text{lease payments}}$	Measures coverage capability more broadly than times interest earned by including lease payments as a fixed expense.

Gross profit margin	$$\frac{\text{Gross profit}}{\text{Net sales}}$$	Measures profit generated after consideration of cost of products sold.
Operating profit margin	$$\frac{\text{Operating profit}}{\text{Net sales}}$$	Measures profit generated after consideration of operating expenses.
Net profit margin	$$\frac{\text{Net earnings}}{\text{Net sales}}$$	Measures profit generated after consideration of all expenses and revenues.
Return on investment	$$\frac{\text{Net earnings}}{\text{Total assets}}$$	Measures overall efficiency of firm in managing assets and generating profits.
Return on equity	$$\frac{\text{Net earnings}}{\text{Stockholders' equity}}$$	Measures rate of return on stockholders' (owners) investment.
Earnings per common share	$$\frac{\text{Net earnings}}{\text{Average common shares outstanding}}$$	Shows return to common stock shareholder for each share owned.
Price/earnings ratio	$$\frac{\text{Market price of common stock}}{\text{Earnings per share}}$$	Expresses multiple that stock market places on a firm's earnings.
Dividend payout ratio	$$\frac{\text{Dividends per share}}{\text{Earnings per share}}$$	Shows percentage of earnings paid to shareholders.
Dividend yield	$$\frac{\text{Dividends per share}}{\text{Market price of common stock}}$$	Shows the rate earned by shareholders from dividends relative to current price of stock.

Accelerated Cost Recovery System: The system established by the Economic Recovery Tax Act of 1981 to simplify depreciation methods for tax purposes and to encourage investment in capital.

Accelerated depreciation: An accounting procedure under which larger amounts of expense are apportioned to the earlier years of an asset's depreciable life and lesser amounts to the later years.

Accounting period: The length of time covered for reporting accounting information.

Accounting principles: The methods and procedures used in preparing financial statements.

Accounts payable: Amounts owed to creditors for items or services purchased from them.

Accounts receivable: Amounts owed to an entity, primarily by its trade customers.

Accounts receivable turnover: *See* Summary of financial ratios (Appendix E).

Accrual basis of accounting: A method of earnings determination under which revenues are recognized in the accounting period when earned, regardless of when cash is received; and expenses are recognized in the period incurred, regardless of when cash is paid.

Accrued liabilities: Obligations resulting from the recognition of an expense prior to the payment of cash.

Accumulated depreciation: A balance sheet account indicating the amount of depreciation expense taken on plant and equipment up to the balance sheet date.

Acid-test ratio: See Summary of financial ratios (Appendix E).

Activity ratio: A ratio that measures the liquidity of specific assets and the efficiency of the firm in managing assets.

Additional paid-in-capital: The amount by which the original sales price of stock shares sold exceeds the par value of the stock.

Allowance for doubtful accounts: The balance sheet account that measures the amount of outstanding accounts receivable expected to be uncollectable.

Amortization: The process of expense allocation applied to the cost expiration of intangible assets.

Annual report: The report to shareholders published by a firm; contains information required by generally accepted accounting principles and/or by specific SEC requirements.

Assets: Items possessing service or use potential to the owner.

Auditor's report: Report by independent auditor attesting to the fairness of the financial statements of a company.

Average collection period: *See* Summary of financial ratios (Appendix E).

Average cost method: A method of valuing inventory and cost of products sold; all costs, including those in beginning inventory, are added together and divided by the total number of units to arrive at a cost per unit.

Balance sheet: The financial statement that shows the financial condition of a company on a particular date.

Balancing equation: Assets = Liabilities + Stockholders' Equity.

Book value: *See* Net book value.

Calendar year: The year starting January 1 and ending December 31.

Capital assets: *See* Fixed assets.

Capital in excess of par value: *See* Additional paid-in-capital.

Capital lease: A leasing arrangement that is, in substance, a purchase by the lessee, who accounts for the lease as an acquisition of an asset and the incurrence of a liability.

Capital structure: The permanent long-term financing of a firm represented by long-term debt, preferred stock, common stock, and retained earnings.

Capitalize: The process whereby initial expenditures are included in the cost of assets and allocated over the period of service.

Cash basis of accounting: A method of accounting under which revenues are recorded when cash is received and expenses are recognized when cash is paid.

Cash conversion cycle: The amount of time (expressed in number of days) required to sell inventory and collect accounts receivable, less the number of days credit extended by suppliers.

Cash equivalents: Security investments that are readily converted to cash.

Cash flow from operations: The amount of cash generated from a business enterprise's normal, ongoing operations during an accounting period.

Commercial paper: Unsecured short-term promissory notes of large companies.

Common size financial statements: A form of financial ratio analysis that allows the comparison of firms with different levels of sales or total assets by introducing a common denominator. A common size balance sheet expresses each item on the balance sheet as a percentage of total assets, and a common size income statement expresses each item as a percentage of net sales.

Common stock: Shares of stock representing ownership in a company.

Complex capital structure: Capital structures including convertible securities, stock options, and warrants.

Conservatism: The accounting concept holding that in selecting among accounting methods the choice should be the one with the least favorable effect on the firm.

Consolidation: The combination of financial statements for two or more separate legal entities when one company, the parent, owns more than 50% of the voting stock of the other company or companies.

Constant dollar approach: An approach to adjust items for inflation by applying the change in a general price index; also called general price level.

Contra-asset account: An account shown as a deduction from the asset to which it relates in the balance sheet.

Convertible securities: Securities that can be converted or exchanged for another type of security, typically common stock.

Cost flow assumption: An assumption regarding the order in which inventory is sold; used to value cost of goods sold and ending inventory.

Cost method: A procedure to account for investments in the voting stock of other companies under which the investor recognizes investment income only to the extent of any cash dividends received.

Cost of goods sold: The cost to the seller of products sold to customers.

Cost of goods sold percentage: The percentage of cost of goods sold to net sales.

Cost of sales: *See* Cost of goods sold.

Cumulative effect of change in accounting principle: The difference in the actual amount of retained earnings at the beginning of the period in which a change in accounting principle is instituted and the amount of retained earnings that would have been reported at that date if the new accounting principle had been applied retroactively for all prior periods.

Cumulative translation adjustment: Adjustment to the equity section of the balance sheet resulting from the translation of foreign financial statements.

Current (assets/liabilities): Items expected to be converted into cash or paid out in cash in one year or one operating cycle, whichever is longer.

Current cost approach: An approach to adjust items for inflation by applying the specific price change of each asset.

Current maturities of long-term debt: The portion of long-term debt that will be repaid during the upcoming year.

Current ratio: *See* Summary of financial ratios (Appendix E).

Debt ratio: *See* Summary of financial ratios (Appendix E).

Debt to equity: *See* Summary of financial ratios (Appendix E).

Deferred method (for investment tax credit): The accounting procedure under which the benefit of the tax credit is spread over the useful life of the asset that generated the credit.

Deferred taxes: The balance sheet account that results from timing differences in the recognition of revenue and expense for taxable income and reported income.

Depletion: The accounting procedure used to allocate the cost of acquiring and developing natural resources.

Depreciation: The accounting procedure used to allocate the cost of an asset, which will benefit a business enterprise for more than a year, over the asset's service life.

Discontinued operations: The financial results of selling a major business segment.

Discretionary items: Items (revenues and expenses) under the control of management with respect to budget levels and timing.

Dividend payout ratio: *See* Summary of financial ratios (Appendix E).

Dividend yield: *See* Summary of financial ratios (Appendix E).

Double-declining balance method: An accounting procedure for depreciation under which the straight-line rate of depreciation is doubled and applied to the net book value of the asset.

Earnings before income taxes: The profit recognized before the deduction of income taxes.

Earnings before interest and taxes (EBIT): The operating profit of a firm.

Earnings per common share: *See* Summary of financial ratios (Appendix E).

Earnings statement: *See* Income statement.

Equity: *See* Stockholders' equity.

Equity method: The procedure used for an investment in common stock when the investor company can exercise significant influence over the investee company; the investor recognizes investment income of the investee's net income in proportion to the percent of stock owned.

Expenses: Costs incurred to produce revenue.

Extraordinary transactions: Items that are unusual in nature and not expected to recur in the foreseeable future.

Financial leverage: The extent to which a firm finances with debt, measured by the relationship between total debt and total assets.

Financial leverage index: The ratio of return on equity to return on assets (adjusted to exclude the effect of the method used to finance assets), which indicates whether financial leverage is being used successfully by a firm. An index greater than 1 indicates the successful use of financial leverage.

Financial ratios: Calculations made to standardize financial data; expressed in terms of mathematical relationships in the form of percentages or times.

Financial statements: Accounting information regarding the financial position of a firm, the results of operations, and the changes in financial position. Four statements comprise the basic set of financial statements: the balance sheet, the income statement, the statement of retained earnings, and the statement of changes in financial position.

Finished goods: Products for which the manufacturing process is complete.

First-in-first-out (FIFO): A method of valuing inventory and cost of goods sold under which the items purchased first are assumed to be sold first.

Fiscal year: A 12-month period starting on a date other than January 1 and ending 12 months later.

Fixed assets: Tangible, long-lived assets that are expected to provide service benefit for more than one year.

Fixed asset turnover: *See* Summary of financial ratios (Appendix E).

Fixed charge coverage: *See* Summary of financial ratios (Appendix E).

Flow-through method (for investment tax credit): The accounting procedure under which the benefit of the tax credit is taken in the year the asset is purchased.

Form 10-K: An annual document filed with the Securities and Exchange Commission by companies that sell securities to the public.

Fully diluted earnings per share: The earnings per share figure calculated using all potentially dilutive securities in the number of shares outstanding.

Funds: Cash or working capital (current assets less current liabilities).

General price level adjustment: An approach used to adjust items for inflation by applying the change in a general price index; also called constant dollar.

Generally accepted accounting principles: The accounting methods and procedures used to prepare financial statements.

Goodwill: An intangible asset representing the unrecorded assets of a firm; appears in the accounting records only if the firm is acquired for a price in excess of the fair market value of its net assets.

Gross margin: *See* Gross profit.

Gross profit: The difference between net sales and cost of goods sold.

Gross profit margin: *See* Summary of financial ratios (Appendix E).

Historical cost: The amount of cash or value of other resources used to acquire an asset; for some assets, historical cost is subject to depreciation, amortization, or depletion.

Income statement: The financial statement presenting the revenues and expenses of a business enterprise for an accounting period.

Industry comparisons: Average financial ratios compiled for industry groups.

Industry segment: *See* segment.

Intangible assets: Assets possessing no physical characteristics but having values to a company's owners.

Interim statements: Financial statements issued for periods shorter than one year.

Inventories: Items held for sale or used in the manufacture of products that will be sold.

Inventory turnover: *See* Summary of financial ratios (Appendix E).

Investment tax credit: A tax credit (direct reduction of taxes paid) provided by tax laws for investment in capital equipment.

Last-in-first-out (LIFO): A method of valuing inventory and cost of goods sold under which the items purchased last are assumed to be sold first.

Leasehold improvement: An addition or improvement made to a leased structure.

Leverage ratio: A ratio that measures the extent of a firm's financing with debt relative to equity and its ability to cover interest and other fixed charges.

Liabilities: Claims against assets.

Line of credit: A prearranged loan allowing borrowing up to a certain maximum amount.

Liquidity: The ability of a firm to generate sufficient cash to meet its cash needs.

Liquidity ratio: A ratio that measures a firm's ability to meet needs for cash as they arise.

Long-term debt: Obligations with maturities longer than one year.

Long-term debt to Total Capitalization: *See* Summary of financial ratios (Appendix E).

Lower of cost or market method: A method of valuing inventory under which cost or market, whichever is lower, is selected for each item, each group, or for the whole inventory.

Management's Discussion and Analysis of the Financial Condition and Results of Operation: A section of the annual report that is required and monitored by the Securities and Exchange Commission in which management presents a detailed coverage of the firm's liquidity, capital resources, and operations.

Marketable securities: Cash not needed immediately in the business and temporarily invested to earn a return.

Matching principle: The accounting principle holding that expenses are to be matched with the generation of revenues in order to determine net income for an accounting period.

Merchandise inventories: Goods purchased for resale to the public.

Minority interest: Claims of shareholders other than the parent company against the net assets and net income of a subsidiary company.

Monetary assets/liabilities: Items that are stated in terms of current value and do not need to be adjusted for inflation; include cash, marketable securities, and all liabilities other than deferred income.

Multiple-step format: A format for presenting the income statement under which several intermediate profit measures are shown.

Net assets: Total assets less total liabilities.

Net book value of capital assets: The difference between original cost of property, plant, and equipment and any accumulated depreciation to date.

Net earnings: The firm's profit or loss after consideration of all revenue and expense reported during the accounting period.

Net income: *See* Net earnings.

Net profit margin: *See* Summary of financial ratios (Appendix E).

Net sales: Total sales revenue less sales returns and sales allowances.

Net trade cycle: *See* Cash conversion cycle.

Net working capital: *See* Working capital.

Noncurrent assets/liabilities: Items expected to benefit the firm for/with maturities of more than one year.

Notes payable: A short-term obligation in the form of a promissory note to suppliers or financial institutions.

Notes to the financial statements: Supplementary information to financial statements that explain the firm's accounting policies and provide detail about particular accounts that require clarification.

Operating cycle: The time required to purchase or manufacture inventory, sell the product, and collect the cash.

Operating expenses: Costs relating to the normal functions of a business.

Operating lease: A rental agreement where no ownership rights are transferred to the lessee at the termination of the rental contract.

Operating profit: Sales revenue less the expenses associated with generating sales. Operating profit measures the overall performance of a company on its normal, ongoing operations.

Operating profit margin: *See* Summary of financial ratios (Appendix E).

Options: *See* Stock options.

Par value: The floor price below which stock cannot be sold initially.

Plant and equipment: *See* Fixed assets.

Preferred stock: Capital stock of a company that carries certain privileges or rights not carried by all outstanding shares of stock.

Prepaid expenses: Expenditures made in the current or prior period that will benefit the firm at some future time.

Price-earnings ratio: *See* Summary of financial ratios (Appendix E).

Primary earnings per share: The earnings per share figure calculated on the assumption that only some of the potentially dilutive securities have been converted into common stock.

Principal: The original amount of a liability.

Prior period adjustment: A change in the retained earnings balance primarily resulting from the correction of errors made in previous accounting periods.

Pro forma financial statements: Projections of future financial statements based on a set of assumptions regarding future revenues, expenses, level of investment in assets, financing methods and costs, and working capital management.

Profitability ratio: A ratio that measures the overall performance of a firm and its efficiency in managing assets, liabilities, and equity.

Property, plant, and equipment: *See* Fixed assets.

Publicly held companies: Companies that operate to earn a profit and issue shares of stock to the public.

Qualified opinion: An opinion rendered by an independent auditor of financial statements stating that the statements in some way do not present fairly the financial position, the results of operations, and/or the changes in financial position for the company.

Quality of financial reporting: A subjective evaluation of the extent to which financial reporting is free of manipulation and accurately reflects the financial condition and operating success of a business enterprise.

Quick ratio: *See* Summary of financial ratios (Appendix E).

Raw materials: Basic commodities or natural resources that will be used in the production of goods.

Replacement cost: The estimated cost of acquiring new and substantially equivalent property at current prices.

Reported income: The net income published in financial statements.

Retained earnings: The sum of every dollar a company has earned since its inception, less any payments made to shareholders in the form of cash or stock dividends.

Return on assets: *See* Return on investment.

Return on equity: *See* Summary of financial ratios (Appendix E).

Return on investment: *See* Summary of financial ratios (Appendix E).

Revenue: The inflow of assets resulting from the sale of goods or services.

Sales allowance: A deduction from the original sales invoice price.

Sales return: A cancellation of a sale.

Salvage value: The amount of an asset estimated to be recoverable at the conclusion of the asset's service life.

Segment: A component of a business enterprise that sells primarily to outside markets and for which information about revenue and profit is accumulated.

Segment identifiable assets: Tangible and intangible assets associated with or used by a segment, including an allocated portion of jointly used assets.

Segment operating expenses: Expenses relating to unaffiliated customers and segment revenue; expenses not directly traceable to segments are allocated to segments on a reasonable basis.

Segment operating profit/loss: Segment revenue less all operating expenses.

Segment revenue: Sales of products and services to unaffiliated customers and intersegment sales, with company transfer prices used to determine sales between segments.

Selling and administrative expenses: Costs relating to the sale of products or services and to the management function of the firm.

Short-term: Generally indicates maturity of less than a year.

Single-step format: A format for presenting the income statement under which all items of revenue are grouped together and then all items of expense are deducted to arrive at net income.

Stated value: The floor price below which stock cannot be sold initially; see also par value.

Statement of changes in financial position: The financial statement that summarizes a firm's financing and investing activities for an accounting period and explains the change in financial position from one period to the next.

Statement of retained earnings: The financial statement that presents the details of the transactions affecting the retained earnings account during an accounting period.

Statement of shareholders' equity: A financial statement that summarizes changes in the shareholders' equity section of the balance sheet during an accounting period.

Stock dividends: The issuance of additional shares of stock to existing shareholders in proportion to current ownership.

Stock options: A contract that conveys the right to purchase shares of stock at a specified price within a specified time period.

Stockholders' equity: Claims against assets by the owners of the business; represents the amount owners have invested including income retained in the business since inception.

Straight-line depreciation: An accounting procedure under which equal amounts of expense are apportioned to each year of an asset's life.

Structural analysis: Analysis looking at the internal structure of a business enterprise.

Summary of financial ratios: *See* Appendix E.

Tangible: Having physical substance.

Taxable income: The net income figure used to determine taxes payable to governments.

Time interest earned: *See* Summary of financial ratios (Appendix E).

Timing differences: Differences between pre-tax accounting income and taxable income caused by reporting items of revenue or expense in one period for accounting purposes and in an earlier or later period for income tax purposes.

Total asset turnover: *See* Summary of financial ratios (Appendix E).

Treasury stock: Shares of a company's stock that are repurchased by the company and not retired.

Trend analysis: Evaluation of financial data over several accounting periods.

Units-of-production method: An accounting method under which depreciation expense is based on actual usage.

Unqualified opinion: An opinion rendered by an independent auditor of financial statements stating that the financial statements present fairly the financial position, the results of operations, and the changes in financial position for the company.

Unrealized gains (losses) on marketable equity securities: The gains (losses) disclosed in the equity section resulting from the accounting rule that requires investments in marketable equity securities to be carried at the lower of cost or market value.

Warrant: A certificate issued by a corporation that conveys the right to buy a stated number of shares of stock at a specified price on or before a predetermined date.

Work in process: Products for which the manufacturing process is only partially completed.

Working capital: The amount by which current assets exceed current liabilities.

Working capital from operations: Funds generated through the firm's normal business activity.

Index